Federica Rasenti

essays by

Laura Andreini
Alessandro Benetti
Alessandro Virgilio Mosetti
Giulia Ricci

T0284052

ON THE ROAD city
Paris

ON THE ROAD
Editor of collection
Laura Andreini

editorial project
Forma Edizioni srl, Florence, Italy
redazione@formaedizioni.it
www.formaedizioni.it

editorial production
Archea Associati

editorial direction
Laura Andreini

author
Federica Rasenti*

editorial staff
Maria Giulia Caliri
Monica Giannini
Giulia Guasti
Chiara Mezzabotta

graphic design
Silvia Agozzino
Isabella Peruzzi
Veronica Paoli

translations
Katy Hannan

texts by
Laura Andreini
Alessandro Benetti
Alessandro Virgilio Mosetti
Giulia Ricci

Andrea Benelli: pp. 68, 130,
150, 158, 172, 192
Maria Giulia Caliri: pp. 64, 102,
148, 180, 198
Monica Giannini: pp. 132, 152,
184, 204-206
Federica Rasenti: pp. 66, 70-100,
104, 110-128, 134-138, 142-146,
154-156, 160, 166-170, 174-178,
182, 188-190, 194-196, 200-202

* **Federica Rasenti**, Cultural designer
and curator, Federica Rasenti
graduated in Architectural Design
from Milan Politecnico in 2015.
Since 2016, she has worked with
the Luca Molinari Studio, dealing
with exhibition curation and
scientific coordination, and integrated
management of cultural events
and projects. She has written articles
for several specialised magazines
such as *Domus, area, Urbano* and
Platform Architecture and Design.
In 2023, her book, *Il progetto
del racconto* was published
by LetteraVentidue.

© 2024 Forma Edizioni srl, Florence

All rights reserved, no part of this publication may
be reproduced in any form or by any means without
the prior written permission of the publisher, without
prejudice to the legal requirements provided for in Art.
68, sub-sections 3, 4, 5 and 6 of Law No. 633 of 22
April 1941

First Edition: May 2024

ISBN 978-88-55210-80-5

© ACANTHE by SIAE 2024
© Architecture-Studio by SIAE 2024
© Dominique Perrault by SIAE 2024
© Emmanuel Cattani by SIAE 2024
© FLC by SIAE 2024
© Fondazione Renzo Piano by SIAE 2024
© Gilbert Lézénès by SIAE 2024
© Jean Nouvel by SIAE 2024
© MVRDV by SIAE 2024
© Pierre Soria by SIAE 2024

Table of contents

Guide as a Tool   4
Paris   5

Political / geographical facts   6
General information   7
Useful tips   8

Paris contra Paris. The capital of Europe: 10
A century of contradictions
Lutetia. Image of a completed city?   12
A minor Paris: the contemporary city as a home   14

Skyline   16

Strategies for visiting Paris   20
Routes   22
Louvre, Luxembourg, Champ de Mars,   24
Champs-Élysées, Marais [1-4, 6-8, 16 arr.]
Arsenal, Montparnasse, Rive Gauche, Bercy   60
[4-5, 12-14 arr.]
Ménilmontant, Villette, Créteil, Noisy-le-Grand   106
[19-20 arr.]
Montmartre, Clichy, Saint-Denis [9, 18 arr.]   140
Boulogne-Billancourt, Neuilly-sur-Seine,   162
Nanterre [16 arr.]
Auteuil, Javel, Paris Saclay [15-16 arr.]   188
Olympic and Paralympic venues   210

Museums   212
Theatres   213
Hotels   214
Restaurants   215
Architectural offices   216

Index by architect   218
Index by project   220

Transport   222

Guidebook as a Tool

On the Road is a collection of contemporary architecture guidebooks whose purpose is to tell about a place, whether a city or larger area, through its architectural works chosen to be visited and experienced directly.

The guidebook has a convenient special jacket that opens into a map marking the location of the architectural works and interesting sites to visit. On the back are miniature images and addresses of the architectural works described in detail within.

The book starts with short essays explaining the city or area's present day and history and outlining possible future scenarios with planned or imminent projects. Each work features a photograph of the whole, an architectural drawing (plan or section), a short description, and facts including architect, type, year of construction, address, website, and how to visit it.

The finest architecture of each city and suggested routes are represented by this collection of not-to-be-missed, "timeless" buildings that uniquely define their settings. General information and useful tips for travelers help them optimize their visits and quickly understand the essence of the place described.

Museums, theatres, restaurants, hotels and a list of top architectural firms working in the city let visitors turn a regular trip into an opportunity for study or work.

Note: The pinpoints outside the maps at the beginning of the itineraries are viewable on the rear of the book jacket.

Paris

Laura Andreini*

In the analyses of the many cities we have been presenting for several years in our On the Road series, we could hardly abstain from exploring Paris, a city where the ancient and contemporary has managed to coexist, and where, unlike many other European capitals, contemporary architecture has been granted considerable room for expression.

In this book, we decided to limit the selection exclusively to contemporary projects mainly built over the past thirty years, with a few exceptions of highly representational projects that have become attractions for millions of tourists, like the Louvre Pyramid by Ieoh Ming Pei and the Centre Pompidou by the Piano-Rogers-Franchini team, as well as some of the most iconic examples of Modernism, which found its origins in France thanks to the practical and intellectual efforts of that generation of architects who, in the years before and after both world wars, launched a new interpretation of architectural criteria.

For this reason, in the general narrative we included the Swiss Pavilion by Le Corbusier and Pierre Jeanneret, the Maison du Brésil by Le Corbusier and Lúcio Costa, and Tristan Tzara's house, by Adolf Loos, because they play an introductory role in understanding the architectural evolution of the city.

In summer 2024, Paris will be the setting for a great event: the 33rd Olympic Games; and for this reason, in this guide, we have selected some of the projects that will be completed in conjunction with the sporting event.

We wanted to understand how the public administration had resolved the issues involving the arrival of a vast number of people – estimated numbers are about 15 million visitors – without undermining the normal functioning of the city.

In the case of the London Olympics in 2012, we were able to see how these large events are able to generate interesting urban redevelopment schemes and increase the infrastructural capacity of the city.

One example in this guide is the Saint-Denis Pleyel railway Station designed by Kengo Kuma, which is part of the far greater Grand Paris Express rail system.

Six routes will guide visitors on a circuit that travels from the centre out towards the suburbs, as far as the southern Saclay area, the hub of the vast university campus and research centre, including projects designed by RPBW, OMA, Grafton Architects, LAN and BRUTHER, among others.

We are delighted to present the reader with this tool for analysing such a complex city, composed of so many different and often contrasting realities, but which has managed to create a harmonious fusion despite the problems typical of a European metropolis. We hope that the selection we have chosen will help you in discovering this wonderful city. *Bon voyage*!

* Laura Andreini is Architect and Associate Professor at DIDA, University of Florence. Co-founder of Studio Archea where she still works, she is also writer and deputy editor for *area* magazine.

Political / geographical facts

country
France

language
french

area code
+33 01

coordinates
48°51'24''N
2°21'07''E

area
105,4 km²

population
2.229.095

density
21.148,91 ab./km²

time zone
UTC+1

city website
it.parisinfo.com

Administrative districts

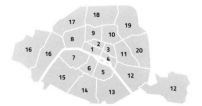

1. Louvre
2. Bourse
3. Temple
4. Hôtel-de-Ville
5. Panthéon
6. Luxembourg
7. Palais-Bourbon
8. Élysée
9. Opéra
10. Entrepôt
11. Popincourt
12. Reuilly / Bois de Vincennes
13. Gobelins
14. Observatoire
15. Vaugirard
16. Passy / Bois de Boulogne
17. Batignolles-Monceau
18. Butte-Montmartre
19. Buttes-Chaumont
20. Ménilmontant

General information
useful addresses and numbers

INFORMATION OFFICES

www.parisinfo.com
29 Rue de Rivoli, Paris
Mon - Sun / 10 am - 6.45 pm

Hôtel de Ville
29 Rue de Rivoli (4 arr.) - M° Hôtel de Ville
Mon - Sun (May-October) / 9 am - 7 pm
Mon - Sun (November-April) / 10 am - 7 pm

Gare du Nord
18 Rue de Dunkerque (10 arr.) -
M° and RER B and D Gare du Nord
Mon - Sun / 8.30 am - 6 pm
except 1 January, 1 May and 25 December

Carrousel du Louvre
99 Rue de Rivoli (1 arr.) - M° Palais Royal -
Musée du Louvre
Mon - Sun / 10 am - 8 pm

Montmartre Visites
1B Cité Germain Pilon
Mon - Sat / 9 am - 7.30 pm
Sun / 4 pm - 7 pm

EMERGENCY SERVICES

Police 17
Fire Department 18
Emergency medical service 15

URBAN TRANSPORT*

Subway, bus, RER, tram

The Paris RATP Metro system is composed of 16 lines
that are identified by a number, colour and direction.
The RER (Réseau Express Régional), together with
the (RATP and SNCF) lines A, B, C, D and E, connects
Paris and the surrounding region. The Bus lines are
numbered and generally run between 6.30 AM and
8.30 PM. Paris and the suburbs are connected by
10 tram lines: T1, T2, T3a, T3b, T4, T5, T6, T7, T8, T11

Taxi
TAXIS G7 3607 (from a French phone number)
+33 1 41 27 66 99 (from a foreign phone number)
Alpha Taxi: +33 1 45 85 85 85
Taxi Blues: +33 8 91 70 10 10

Bicycle rentals
6clo, Paris Bike Tour, Paris à Vélo

EMBASSY OF THE UNITED STATES
2 Avenue Gabriel
+33 (0)1 43 12 22 22

EMBASSY OF THE PEOPLE'S REPUBLIC OF CHINA
20 Rue Monsieur

EMBASSY OF THE UNITED KINGDOM
35 Rue du Faubourg Saint-Honoré
+33 (0)1 44 51 31 00

EMBASSY OF SPAIN
6 Rue Greuze

EMBASSY OF ITALY
51 Rue de Varenne

HOW TO PHONE

From a local landline: Just dial the number, including
the city code (01)

From a foreign landline: Dial the international code
(+33), city code (1) and number

* Ticket types:
  Single tickets t+ €1.90 (zones 1 and 2).
  Book of 10 tickets: € 14.90 or € 7.45
  for children up to 10 years old

Useful tips

1. Paris offers a vast selection of accommodation ranging from **art and design hotels** in the city centre, an endless list of handy **Bed and Breakfasts** spread all over the French capital and iconic luxury hotels. They range from the quintessential **Hôtel Ritz**, whose facade was designed by Jules Hardouin Mansart, the father of the French Baroque style, through to the Mob House, created by the French designer and architect, Philippe Starck, not forgetting the Bulgari Hotel by Italian designer, Citterio-Viel. The French architect, India Mahdavi, created the internal design of the Hotel Thoumieux, while the Hotel Bienvenue interiors were by Chloé Nègre.

2. The quickest and cheapest way to visit Paris is to use the extensive public transport system, especially the Metro, opened in 1900 to celebrate the Universal Exposition. Today its network has 301 stations. The architecture and access structures to the Paris Metro stations have always been created with great attention to design and construction; The most famous are those built in Art Nouveau style, designed in the early 1900s by the artist, Hector Guimard, most of which are still preserved today. As well as the **Metro,** there are five **RER** railway lines that cross Paris connecting up with the outskirts of the city. They can also be used in combination with the Metro in the city centre. There are different systems for buying tickets and travel passes; a particularly handy system is the Paris Visite travel pass that gives access to all transport systems in the city centre for rapid easy travel with maximum freedom.

3. The city administration has worked with the French capital's urban policy over recent years creating incentives to encourage sustainable bicycle mobility as far as possible. In fact, another excellent way to travel around the city is by **bicycle.** The public bike-sharing platform for short-term rentals is called Vélib' Métropole, but there are many companies, some private, that offer bike rental and bike touring options. The Vélopolitain, or more correctly, Plan Vélo Métropolitain, according to its official name, is a long-term plan aimed at reinforcing current infrastructures and developing an efficient network of interconnected and widespread cycling lanes. The idea was set up during the 2020 pandemic. These interventions are part of a wider plan set up by the municipal administration to reduce urban emissions and air pollution. This project will help to partially redefine the appearance and structure of the city: for the moment, the plan foresees nine lines that will cover 70 metropolitan districts, with a total of 215 km of bicycle routes.

4. Like all main European capitals Paris also has integrated **car-sharing** services provided by various companies, to ensure travel possibilities 24 hours day. While we do not advise car travel inside the city, it is a good solution when visiting outside the urban area.

5. Visitors who are interested in learning more about the architectural history and more recent events which are part of the town planning and urban development of Paris should visit the **Pavillon de l'Arsenal**. The institution is housed in a late 19th century building and is home to a cultural centre containing archives, a library, and exhibition spaces that document and narrate the architectural history and more recent projects that are part of the urban fabric of Paris. The Pavillon de l'Arsenal was opened in 1988, and is located in the historic centre (21 Boulevard Morland, 75004, Paris) near the Bastille Metro station. A permanent exhibition, *Paris, the city, and its projects* illustrates the constant evolution of the urban panorama, and a space covering about 800 square metres narrates the birth, development and future prospects underway in the French capital.

Paris contra Paris. The capital of Europe:
A century of contradictions

Alessandro Benetti*

Paris could be conceived as the symbolic capital of Europe. More so than Brussels, the bureaucratic nerve centre, or Berlin, torn apart in the 20th century, or London, offside since Brexit; more than Rome or Athens and their too distant glorious past. The city of the Kings of France, the Revolution, and of more recently elected "sovereigns", General de Gaulle and President Mitterrand, Paris is today, more than ever, the heart of a continent that aspires to champion the inclusive and sustainable democratic principles of the West. From the early 1900s to the present day, a design culture based on these values has been inscribed, not without contradiction, in all three dimensions of the French capital. Through certain antithetical pairs, these brief comments describe some of the lines of force that have influenced the transformations of the last 120 years, the approximate time span between the Haussmann period and that of today.

First of all, solids and voids, with the latter painfully carving its space through the former. At the beginning of the century, the *îlots insalubres* (unhealthy city blocks) were numbered and coloured in red on public hygiene office map, and were destined to be razed to the ground and rebuilt. Their destruction gave rise to visions of a radically Modernist city like that of Le Corbusier for *îlot* 6 (1937), then later in the fifties and sixties, to more solid and pragmatic, standardised *ville au kilomètre* – the tower and slab constructions of Belleville, Place d'Italie and many others. Finally, from the ashes of the most central and notorious *îlot*, number 1, rose the most revolutionary piece of French architecture of the latter 20th century: the Centre Pompidou (1971-77), the disconcerting proto-high-tech structure by the Renzo Piano-Richard Rogers-Gianfranco Franchini team.

Construction and destruction were interwoven in and outside the *îlots* in 20th century Paris. First of all, in August 1971, just a stone's throw from the Centre Pompidou, the destruction of the cast iron and glass Les Halles structure designed by Victor Baltard (1857-74) provoked one of the most controversial and deplored demolitions of 20th century Europe. Immortalised as an immense hole in the Weird Western *Don't Touch the White Woman* by Marco Ferreri (1974), it was then promptly filled in with the RER suburban railway station and a shopping mall. The quarter of Les Halles is the epicentre of a city that ravages and rebuilds on top of itself in peace-time. On this specific site, Claude Vasconi, Georges Pencreac'h and Jean Willerval designed their timidly postmodern *parapluies* (1974-84) followed by the gentler *Canopée* by Patrick Berger, opened in 2016, and already a little past its prime.

The barycentre between Centre Pompidou and Les Halles, is the Boulevard de Sébastopol, the cardo of Haussmann's Paris, Cartesian in its attempt to replace the disorder of the past with uniform and carefully sequenced facades. Despite being a great rationalist, Haussmann warned that "there is no reason to destroy all the houses in a city simply to rebuild them in another form and to make the streets look better". And, in fact, following the downfall of the Baron, Paris was built in the midst of ongoing conflict between the respect and rejection

* Alessandro Benetti is an Architect, PhD in History of Modern and Contemporary Architecture and Research Assistant at Politecnico di Torino. He collaborates with *Domus* and he is editor-in-chief of *Urbano*. Over the last few years, his researches have focused on the 20th century *rénovation urbaine* in Eastern Paris and on French seaside modernist architectures. He is a member of the Board of Directors of ANCSA, the Italian Association for Historic-Artistic Centers.

of his conventions. There was a battle against his *plafond* (literally: urban ceiling) contradicting it with dozens of late-Modernist towers, from the austere Tour Croulebarbe designed by Edouard Albert (1958-60) to the extravagant Orgues de Flandre by Martin van Treeck (1970-80). Rigorous street alignment was rejected in favour of three dimensional assemblage, such as the experiments by Roger Anger, Mario Heyman and Pierre Puccinelli in the 1960s – until the facade finally disappeared entirely with the transparency of the Fondation Cartier (1991-94), perhaps the most successful of Jean Nouvel's urban designs. Research was carried out for updated spatial and formal regulation for the ZAC Rive Gauche (1990s), that Christian de Portzamparc resolved with replicated *îlots ouverts* (open blocks) aligned along street fronts, but open and accessible. On the contrary in more recent districts like the ZAC Clichy-Batignolles (from 2000) the approach became an Esperanto of volumes, styles and materials, where disparate housing and office blocks rose impatiently around the park by François Grether, Jacqueline Osty and OGI, in the shade of the totemic Law Court complex by Renzo Piano (2012-20). In Batignolles and other quarters, Paris remained a city of monuments and public spaces; monuments became transparent and open spaces were often conceived as zero volume architecture. The brilliant Arab World Institute by Jean Nouvel (1981-87), decorated with his openable *mashrabiya*, the Louvre Pyramid by I.M. Pei (1985-89), and the four towers of Dominique Perrault's monumental National Library of France (1989-96), triumph of Mitterrand-style welfare policy, are all transparent. On the contrary, Bernard Tschumi's Parc de la Villette (1982-98) dense with raised walkways and carmine-red follies, and the new Place de la République by TVK (2010-13), a very busy urban roof-terrace built over the metro station, are three-dimensional in concept and function.

In conclusion, Paris remains a magnetic centre in a precarious balance with its regional and national surroundings, always at risk of 'desertification' despite continuous efforts to decentralise the city. The first to emerge outside the administrative-infrastructural boundaries of the *périphérique* ring road were the high-rise housing projects of the fifties and sixties, including some designed by excellent modernists like Émile Aillaud, Jean Dubuisson and Fernand Pouillon. They were followed by the *new towns* of the seventies and eighties, an important moment of reflection on the urban morphology that found its peak in the unachieved project by OMA for Melun Sénart (1987). More recently, public transport systems accentuate its regional scale with the Grand Paris Express stations that become poles of densification, urbanism, and gentrification. Finally, even the Olympic Village coordinated by Perrault for the 2024 games, is spread over three municipalities in the inner ring suburbs. Many examples are not mentioned in this short and incomplete commentary, a rapid ride through the complexity of 120 years of history of a European metropolis. Even so, readers will discover them all in the detailed descriptions that follow, where they will find examples of the topics mentioned here, and above all, in the streets of Paris, capital of Europe.

Lutetia. Image of a completed city?

Alessandro Virgilio Mosetti*

The city enclosed within the circular infrastructure of the Boulevard Périphérique emerged clad in an "urban facade", immediately recognisable and of recent construction: "Old Paris is no more – the form of a city changes more quickly, alas! than the human heart", wrote Charles Baudelaire in *The Swan,* in 1860, when describing the *grands travaux* promoted under the reign of Napoleon III by the Prefect, Georges Eugène Haussmann, hydraulic engineer, Eugène Belgrand and landscape architect, Jean-Charles Adolphe Alphand. In his book, *The Kill,* Émile Zola stated that the urban fabric of the pre and post Revolution medieval city seemed to have been "slashed with sabre cuts".

In the mid-19th century the facade of the middle-class urban areas was modelled on elements of the pre-existant city in all scales of intervention: the 74 kilometres of new road layouts were arranged in a hierarchy of first and second rank streets; residential buildings were established according to type; city blocks were enclosed, connected with public spaces by means of continuous unified frontages: (*rue-mur*); building fronts became homogeneous, based on the prototype of those built in the Rue de Rivoli a few decades earlier. On a larger scale, arrondissements were equipped with public services, squares and parks. As a consequence, a new underground infrastructure, a 300 kilometre sewage network, was built. The design of new urban spaces was the modern interpretation of the Royal Squares of the *Ancien Régime*; the new monuments of the Second Empire (theatres, hospitals, government buildings) were isolated and framed perspectively by *boulevards* and *avenues.* These routes either continued the pre-existing road layout or created new axes aimed at facilitating urban traffic in a north-south direction (from Boulevard de Sébastopol to Boulevard Saint-Michel) and east-west (with the extension of Rue de Rivoli aligned with the 17th century Avenue des Champs-Élysées). The direction of these two axes was not moved far from the original *cardo* (the current Rue Saint-Martin on the Right Bank, and Rue Saint-Jacques on the Left Bank) and the *decumanus* of *Lutetia Parisiorum.* The new main routes defined a modern urban crossroads at Place du Châtelet reinstating the continuous reciprocal connection that existed between the two banks of the Seine in the heart of the Merovingian-Roman core (between the Marais, the Île de la Cité and the Latin Quarter). The new axes focussed on the city, breaking through the last bastion of the Thiers walls (Paris fortifications) and anticipating the urban expansion of the *Grand Paris* project (still under construction today).

The middle class facade was continued in a different style from the Parisian models built from the 17th century; buildings were enhanced, varied in scale, and systematically replicated to create spatial, aesthetic and formal solutions for a capital city associated with the second industrial revolution and the belief in social hygiene as an answer to pauperism. As a result of these convictions, the image of the city was so praiseworthy that Paris became a prototype to be replicated in other cities and an efficient example of urban renewal.

* Alessandro Virgilio Mosetti is an Architect and Research Doctor in Architectural Composition. He has written essays and articles for Italian and international magazines and teaches and tutors for the Architectural Composition Curriculum in doctoral studies at the IUAV University in Venice. He has worked with the Luca Molinari Studio since 2022, collaborating on editorial projects, consulting and curating work in the field of architecture.

This "city-worksite" formed the backdrop for the characters in Zola's books: *Les Rougon-Macquart,* as well as other works by Baudelaire, Flaubert, and after construction completion, by Walter Benjamin in his *Arcades Project.* These characters, real or imaginary, were in search of what remained of the pre-Haussmann city, with its dense irregular urban fabric. In his *Belly of Paris,* Zola described what was later echoed in Italo Calvino's docufilm *Un uomo invisibile* [Invisible Man] (1974) directed, as if from a stratigraphic window, onto the origins of the city, and the abyss of the excavation of the Forum des Halles, on the same site that had housed the twelve covered market pavilions designed by Victor Baltard in 1872.

The worksite of the 19th century "facade" limited (and still limits) the intervention objectives and processes of modern contemporary projects within the fabric of the historic centre. The issue of urban voids left by Haussmann's design became an opportunity for projects (as in the case of the unhealthy city block on which, a century later, the Centre Pompidou was built). This also applies to on-site demolition and reconstruction (Les Halles) or the restructuring of large 19th century urban parks (Parc de la Villette). This restrictive but successful image of Paris-*Lutetia* is rooted in collective memory; it was put into construction just as it was imagined. Where will the city be completed today?

Outside the Périphérique, the "facade" does not exist. The *banlieue* is an honest depiction as the double of the city from which it evolved as a consequence. It absorbed the problems expelled from the 19th-20th century city, and with a greater degree of freedom, experimented with new urban settlement models in an attempt to establish an image with its own identity, but integrated with the city within the walls. Today, this is where the *Grand Paris* will be built.

A minor Paris: the contemporary city as a home

Giulia Ricci*

In recent years the French capital has shed its skin, changing its aspect rapidly and very visibly. This process was widely covered in the media, including the general press, which did not limit coverage to simple features on *pop up* cycle lanes during the pandemic. Already in November 2014, the newly-elected mayor, Anne Hidalgo and deputy mayor, Jean-Louis Missika[1] launched *Réinventer Paris*, a new call for urban project bids open to both architects and the general public. Missika justified the operation as a break from the conservative methods of local developers, in attempt to generate innovative ideas.

This initiative became an exportable model travelling around the world with the C40 Cities Climate Leadership Group. In 2015 Hidalgo launched the *Plan Vélo*, to reinforce and expand cycling networks in urban (REVe) and regional areas (RER-Vélo), today called Vélo Île-de-France, which hopes to reach 750 kms of cycling lanes by 2030. The same year, the public administration adopted the "15 minute city" plan by Carlos Moreno during the COP21 meeting: a sustainable urban planning concept that envisaged the proximity of essential services such as work and leisure activities within a short distance from home, to reduce car travel. The administration, now in its second mandate, became the international pioneer for the implementation of an ecological vision of the city with a series of targeted policies. Returning to 2014, however, Hidalgo declared[2] that housing would be the absolute priority of her mandate. Today, the housing crisis present in European and North American cities exists in Paris as well. Despite this problem, today the capital provides access to public housing to a quarter of its residents and supports small-sized businesses on neighbourhood scale. This policy has resulted in creating more socially mixed districts, even within the Boulevard Périphérique, and is aimed at protecting those workers who generate prosperity for the city like "teachers, healthcare workers, nurses, university students, bakers and butchers"[3].

The attention focussed on housing has generated experiments into multi-family residences, often with very high quality results. Alongside the municipal initiatives, there are also different enterprises, including Régie immobilière de la Ville de Paris (RIVP), Elogie Siemp and Paris Habitat (the largest public building body in Europe) as well as public operations that involve private participation, like the Zones d'Aménagement Concerté (ZAC) established in 1967.

Testimony to the quality of this production, in 2021, Anne Lacaton and Jean-Philippe Vassal were awarded the Pritzker Architecture Prize for their work in "giving priority to improving human living conditions […], able to provide social, ecological, and economic advantages for individuals, and fostering urban evolution". Among some of their social housing projects, the prize was awarded for two specific interventions in Paris: the restoration of the Tour Bois-le-Prêtre (2011, 17th arr., for Paris Habitat), built in 1961 by Raymond Lopez, and the Ourcq-Jaurès student and social housing units (2014, 19th arr., for Siemp). This concept spread throughout the country and especially in Paris,

* Giulia Ricci is a professional journalist, and on the editorial staff at *Domus* since 2018. Since 2022, she has written with CTS Cultura della Fondazione OAMi and is an advisor for the EU Mies Awards, Italian Prize for Architecture and Gubbio Prize. She has written for *OASE journal*, *ARK* and *Largo Duomo*; and books like *Milano e le università* (2024).

where many examples, all very different in design, context, and scale, are often equipped with services for the local community. One of the core projects will be focussed on adapting existing structures, a key strategy for reaching 40% of accessible housing units by 2035. Among these, close to the Musée d'Orsay, are the 254 units in the îlot Saint-Germain (2024, 7th arr., for RIVP) by FBAA and h2o architectes. They are constructed in three 18th century and 1960s buildings, which previously housed the Ministry of Defense, and the Reuilly military barracks (2021, 12th arr., for Paris Habitat). It is a 40,000 square metre densification intervention of a 19th century structure designed by a group guided by h2o architectes. The project designs are by LIN Architects, Anyoji Beltrando, Charles-Henri Tachon, NP2F + OFFICE Kersten Geers David Van Severen, MIR architectes and Lacroix Chessex.

Other examples develop difficult plots, such as the Social Housing Pelleport (2016, XX arr.) by BRUTHER or the Résidence Julia Bartet (2018, 14th arr.) by Charles-Henri Tachon, close to railway structures. The relationship with infrastructures is also a feature in the Residence for Researchers Julie-Victoire Daubié (2018, 14th arr., for RIVP), again by BRUTHER, near the Boulevard Périphérique, and the Ferme du Rail project by Grand Huit (2019, 19th arr., for *Réinventer Paris*), combining the residential project with an urban agricultural plan. This functional mix also occurs in Stendhal (2017, 20th arr., RIVP) by Studio Muoto, with 35 housing units, a nursery school, and a refuge shelter. Among the student residences, is the striking project Chris Marker student housing by Experience (2017, 14th arr.), that includes the recovery of an RATP bus depot, and the complex by BRUTHER and Baukunst at Paris-Saclay (2020).

These examples are simply a part of the patrimony produced by local and international firms, ranging from SANAA social housing (2018, 16th arr., for Paris Habitat), to the invention of new methods such as the Common House project by the French-Chilean firm, Plan Común (2023, Pantin). This focus on housing has two aspects: the first is the public policy carried out on a vast scale, while the second reveals all the specific interventions that range from architectural projects to spontaneous initiatives by the public, the result of an increase in urban awareness. This dialogue has helped link up different scales and certain *ad hoc* systems over the years, like the Pavillon de l'Arsenal (1988, 4th arr.), the first information and exhibition centre for urban topics (*urban centre*) in Europe. Together, these activities are able to generate a "minor Paris"[4], in other words, they can weave the fabric of a city that can become a home.

1. Until 2020, Jean-Louis Missika was deputy mayor, in charge of urban planning, architecture, the Greater Paris projects, economic development and attraction.
2. K. Willsher, "'My absolute priority is housing,' says Paris' first female mayor", *www.latimes.com*, 27 July 2014.
3. T. Fuller, "How Does Paris Stay Paris? By Pouring Billions Into Public Housing", *www.nytimes.com*, 17 March 2024.
4. A reference to *Venezia Minore*, a book by Egle Renata Trincanato in 1948. The publication described research on Venice by the architect and professor of urban planning at IUAV university, on town planning and residential problems in the lagoon towns, excluding monumental buildings.

Tour Eiffel

Les Invalides

Church of
Saint-Germain-des-Prés

Ministère de l'Agriculture

Trocadéro

Basilique Sainte-Clotilde-et-Sainte-Valère

Université Paris Cité

Pont Saint-Michel

© Sasha Kahn / AdobeStock

Tours Aillaud

Grande Arche
de La Défense

Tour D2

Esplanade du Général de Gaulle

© Alfonsodetomas / AdobeStock

Strategies for visiting Paris

It could seem paradoxical and almost contradictory to map out specific directions for the very city in which the term *flânerie* was first invented and defined. In the late19th century, Baudelaire coined this term to describe the activity of the *flâneur*, later confirmed by Walter Benjamin; it consists of wandering casually around the city without a precise route or objective, acquiring an analytical reading of the space, and allowing oneself to become surprised by the unexpected. To describe the duration of this urban observation tour could seem unpredictable and subjective, a mission that is all the more complex in the Paris of today, where layers of architectural history accumulated over centuries have absorbed the lessons of modernity, leaving the place free for a contemporary city in constant evolution.

In our guide, we have narrowed the field of our architectural profiles, preferring a partial synopsis of the modern contemporary city, through the 20th and early 21st centuries.

We cannot claim that our descriptions are all-inclusive, but the itineraries will enable visitors to discover the macro-areas of the city; the routes have been designed more as anchor points for a potentially, more widespread exploration.

Given the absence of certain aspects of the city established by the organic narrative in this guide, some examples of pre-20th century architecture that are not included in the profiles will be briefly described in the paragraphs below. They provide further reference points that may be useful as a guide for one of the many possible visits in the city.

Itinerary A | Louvre, Luxembourg, Champ de Mars, Champs-Élysées, Marais [1-4, 6-8, 16 arr.]
In this very central part of the city, set between the Champ de Mars, Arc de Triomphe and the Medieval quarter of the Marais, the route covers both banks of the Seine. This area has the highest concentration of museums in Paris, including the world's most visited museum: the Louvre. The itinerary includes crossing over to the I'Île de la Cité, the historical heart of the city and its geographical centre. Of special note are the two Gothic masterpieces: the cathedral of Notre Dame and Sainte-Chapelle; the Conciergerie, part of the ancient Palais de la Cité, the centre of Royal power between the X and XIV centuries, plus Place Dauphine, at the end of the island near the Pont Neuf.

Itinerary B | Arsenal, Montparnasse, Rive Gauche, Bercy [4-5, 12-14 arr.]
The second route follows on from the first, towards the southern side of the city between the Jardin du Luxembourg and the external ring road, the Boulevard Périphérique. Here visitors must not miss the obligatory stroll through the Latin Quarter, the intellectual centre of Medieval Paris, and still home to the Sorbonne, the prestigious Parisian university. This area was only marginally

affected by the Haussman demolitions during the creation of the Boulevard Saint-Michel and Boulevard Saint-Germain, leaving the medieval aspect of the quarter almost intact.

Itinerary C | Ménilmontant, Villette, Créteil, Noisy-le-Grand [19-20 arr.]
The third route is different as it covers a large area to the west of the city, from Porte de la Chapelle to Porte de Vincennes, and includes two extra-urban excursions to Créteil and Noisy-le-Grand. To reach this area, spreading from the city centre to the more distant outskirts, visitors must cross a symbolic convergence point, the Place de la République, located at the intersection between the 3rd, 10th, and 11th arrondissements.

Itinerary D | Montmartre, Clichy, Saint-Denis [9, 18 arr.]
This route covers the northern area of the city, beginning at Pigalle, crossing Montmartre and continuing towards the outer districts of Clichy and Saint-Denis. Two fundamental architectural landmarks mark the beginning and end of this route: the Opéra Garnier, in the 19th arrondissement, designed by Charles Garnier between 1861 and 1975, and at the other end, the Basilica of Saint-Denis, an outstanding example of French Gothic style, restored between 1846 and 1879 by Eugène Viollet-le-Duc.

Itinerary E | Boulogne-Billancourt, Neuilly-sur-Seine, Nanterre [16 arr.]
Following a route along the north-west side of the city from the Bois de Boulogne, this itinerary is almost entirely located in the Hauts-de-Seine department, outside the Paris urban area, with a special focus on the financial district of La Défense in Nanterre. This could be described as the most architecturally homogeneous area of Paris, thanks to a regeneration and modernisation project that began in the 1970s; it now features the greatest concentration of contemporary architecture in the metropolitan area.

Itinerary F | Auteuil, Javel, Paris Saclay [15-16 arr.]
This final area could be classified as a double itinerary: one covers the most external area to the west of the city, Auteuil and Javel, while the other is closely focussed on the Paris Saclay district, further south-west, about 20 kilometres outside the city limits, and which can be reached by public transport. We considered it important to make this trip outside the city to highlight the large number of contemporary projects created for or linked with the Paris-Saclay University Campus, and the consequential overall redevelopment of the area.

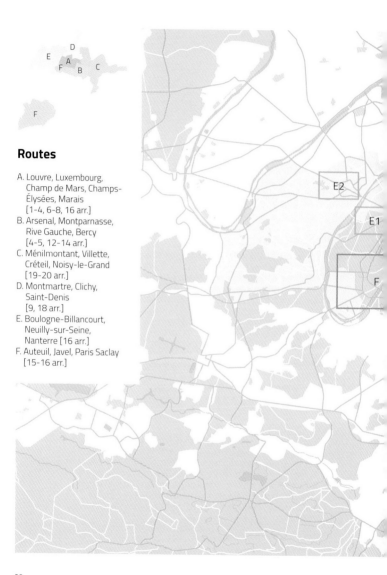

Routes

A. Louvre, Luxembourg,
   Champ de Mars, Champs-
   Élysées, Marais
   [1-4, 6-8, 16 arr.]
B. Arsenal, Montparnasse,
   Rive Gauche, Bercy
   [4-5, 12-14 arr.]
C. Ménilmontant, Villette,
   Créteil, Noisy-le-Grand
   [19-20 arr.]
D. Montmartre, Clichy,
   Saint-Denis
   [9, 18 arr.]
E. Boulogne-Billancourt,
   Neuilly-sur-Seine,
   Nanterre [16 arr.]
F. Auteuil, Javel, Paris Saclay
   [15-16 arr.]

0 m   100 m   250 m

Musée des Arts Dècoratifs

Palais Royal
Musée du Louvre

Arc de Triomphe
du Carrousel

Rue de Rivoli

Seine

Quai des Tuileries

Pyramide
du Louvre

10

Musée du Louvre

Gare du Musée d'Orsay

01

Musée d'Orsay

Quai François Mitterrand

Rue de Lille

Pont Royal

Pont du Carrousel

Quai Voltaire

Rue de l'Université

Rue de Verneuil

Rue du Bac

Rue de Beaune

Rue de Lille

Quai Malaquais

Pont des Arts

Quai de Conti

Rue des Saints-Pères

Statue de la République

Institut de France

Rue de Verneuil

Maison de
L'Amérique Latine

Rue de l'Université

Galerie Maeght

Carré Rive Gauche

Monnaie de Paris

Rue Bonaparte

Galerie Claude Bernard

5

Rue du Bac

Rue Visconti

Rue Mazarine

Rue Gue

Rue du Bac

Rue Perronet

Rue Jacob

Rue de Seine

Boulevard Saint-Germain

Bernard Tschumi Architects

Musée Maillol Paris

Rue de Grenelle

Musée Eugene Delacroix

02

Rue des Saints-Pères

Rue du Dragon

Église de Saint
Germain des Prés

Saint-Germain-des-Prés

Rue Saint-André de

Boulevard Raspail

Rue de Rennes

Rue du Four

Mabillon

Le Procope

Boulevard Raspail

Rue de Sèvres

Musée - Librarie
du Compagnonnage

Odéo

Rue de Babylone

Rue de Sèvres

Théâtre du Vieux-Colombier

Rue Guisarde

Breizh Café

Square
Boucicaut

Saint-Sulpice

Rue Saint-Sulpice

Rue de Sèvres

Boulevard Raspail

Rue du Cherche Midi

Rue de Rennes

Rue de Mézières

Église
Saint-Sulpice

Rue Palatine

Rue Garancière

Rue de Tournon

Rue de Condé

Rue de l'Odéon

Rue Bonaparte

03

Louvre, Luxembourg, Champ de Mars, Champs-Élysées, Marais
[1-4, 6-8, 16 arr.]

01. Musée d'Orsay
02. Maison de Verre
03. Maison des Sciences de l'Homme
04. Meditation Space UNESCO
05. Australian Embassy
06. Site Tour Eiffel
07. Musée du Quai Branly

A1

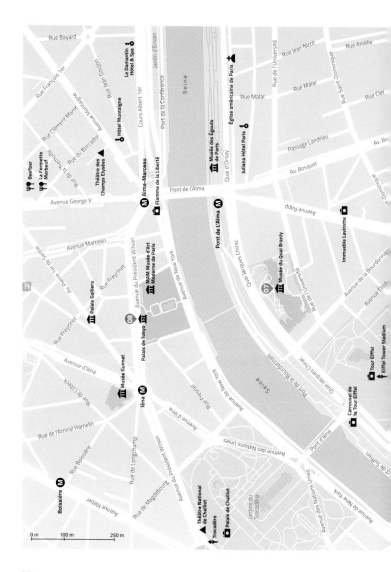

Rue Bayard

Rue François 1er

Rue Clément Marot

Rue du Boccador

Rue Jean Goujon

Rue de la Trémoille

Avenue Montaigne

Beerbar ᵂ♥
La Fermette ᵂ♥
Marbeuf

Théâtre des ▲
Champs Elysées

Le Damantin ⚲
Hôtel & Spa

Hôtel Montaigne ⚲

Jardin d'Erwan

Cours Albert 1er

Pont de la Conférence

Rue de l'Université

Rue Jean Nicot

Rue Amélie

Rue Saint-Dominique

Église américaine de Paris ✚

Rue Malar

Rue Malar

Rue Cler

Av. B

Avenue George V

Ⓜ Alma-Marceau

⛲ Flamme de la Liberté

Seine

Musée des Égouts 🏛
de Paris

Quai d'Orsay

Juliana Hôtel Paris ⚲

Passage Landrieu

Av. Bosquet

Avenue Marceau

MAM Musée d'Art 🏛
Moderne de Paris

Ⓜ Pont de l'Alma

Quai Jacques Chirac

Pont de l'Alma

Rue Rapp

Immeuble Lavirotte ᵒ

H

Palais Galliera 🏛

Rue Freycinet

Av. Pierre 1er de Serbie

Avenue du Président Wilson

Avenue de New York

Palais de Tokyo 🏛 QB

Rue Freycinet

Avenue d'Iéna

Musée Guimet 🏛

Rue de Liberté

Ⓜ Iéna

Rue de l'Amiral Hamelin

Avenue d'Iéna

Rue Freycinet

Avenue de New York

Port de la Bourdonnais

Quai Jacques Chirac

Rue de l'Université

🏛 Musée du Quai Branly

Avenue de la Bourdonnais

Avenue Élég

Seine

Avenue de la Bourdonnais

Tour Eiffel ✝
Eiffel Tower Stadium

Rue Boissière

Rue de Longchamp

Carrousel de ◻
la Tour Eiffel

Ⓜ Boissière

Avenue Kléber

Rue de Magdebourg

Avenue du Président Wilson

Théâtre National ▲
de Chaillot

Palais de Chaillot ◻

🕇 Trocadéro

Jardins du
Trocadéro

Avenue des Nations Unies

Pont d'Iéna

Rue de Suffren

Avenue de New York

Avenue des Nations Unies

0 m   100 m   250 m

A2

Louvre, Luxembourg, Champ de Mars, Champs-Élysées, Marais
[1-4, 6-8, 16 arr.]

08. Palais de Tokyo – extension
09. Apple Store Champs-Élysées
10. Museé du Louvre (Pyramid and Department of Islamic Arts)
11. La Samaritaine
12. Bourse de Commerce – Pinault Collection
13. Atelier Brâncuși
14. Centre Georges Pompidou
15. Fondation d'Entreprise Galeries Lafayette

01. Musée d'Orsay

Esplanade Valéry Giscard d'Estaing
75007 Paris

Tue   Wed, Fri - Sun /
9.30 am - 6 pm
Thu / 9.30 am - 9.45 pm
+33 (0)1 40 49 48 14

www.musee-orsay.fr

 12 > Solférino,
Assemblée Nationale

 RER C > Musée d'Orsay

 68, 69, 73 >
Musée d'Orsay
68, 69, 87, N01 >
Henry de Montherlant
68, 69 > Pont Royal -
Quai Voltaire

Opened on December 1st, 1986, the former Paris railway station redevelopment project, designed by Italian architect Gae Aulenti, represented an innovation and an avant-garde concept. In the 1980s, at a time when the dismantling of the industrial and infrastructural heritage in urban centres was still largely an uncharted area, the idea of restoring this type of structure to house a museum was considered an ingenious solution to preserve collective memory and to create a cultural space for the public. The architect decided not to modify the monumental interior of the Gare D'Orsay station, designed by Victor Laloux for the 1900 Paris Exposition, and focussed on redesigning the internal space to create a new type of museum display layout. The vast central vaulted space, that had previously housed railway lines and platforms, became the main gallery, framed by two clock towers that act as a visual terminus at each end of the exhibition itinerary. The route winds through a series of mainly regular modular blocks that divide up the vast main hall which would have been difficult to fully utilise otherwise. The museum tour flows through three different levels that house works by artists active in the second half of the 19th century through till 1914, including Cézanne, Degas and van Gogh.

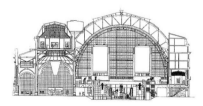

© Jan Kranendonk / AdobeStock

architects
Gae Aulenti

type
cultural

construction
1986

02. Maison de Verre

31 Rue Saint-Guillaume
75007 Paris

open to the public
by appointment
+33 (0)1 45 44 91 21
mdv31@orange.fr

 10, 12 > Sevres -
Babylone
4 > Saint-Germain-
des-Prés
12 > Rue de Bac

 63, 87, N02 >
Saint-Guillaume
68, 83, 94 >
Sèvres - Babylone
63, 68, 83, 84, 94 >
Charlotte Perriand

Built between 1927 and 1931 by the architects Pierre Chareau and Bernard Bijvoet, the Maison de Verre rightly deserves its inclusion among the historic monuments of Parisian Modernism, and is the architect's only surviving building. Concealed from the street, the building sits inside a courtyard at 31, Rue Saint-Guillaume in the 7th arrondissement. The architect and the owners, the Dalsace family, had intended the whole building to assume the appearance of a luminous box, but since they were not able to buy the top floor of the existing building, Chareau invented a different strategy, and grafted a new building onto the existing structure, completely readapting the design in the three floors below. The facade on the courtyard side is clad with translucent glass blocks inserted into a steel structure and still today, it is surmounted by the top floor apartment, inconsistent in its composition and finish. In his role as interior designer, Chareau also created the furnishings and lighting fixtures, a "complete work of art", which had a strong influence on all the details of the iconic residence and medical practice of the Dalsace family.

© Subrealistsandu CC BY-SA 3.0

architects
Pierre Chareau,
Bernard Bijvoet

type
residential

construction
1931

03. Maison des Sciences de l'Homme

54 Boulevard Raspail
75006 Paris

Mon - Fri / 8.30 am - 7.30 pm
+33 (0)1 40 48 64 00
contact@msh-paris.fr
www.fmsh.fr

10, 12 > Sevres -
Babylone
12 > Rennes

68, 94 > Rue du
Cherche Midi
63, 70, 84, 86 >
Sèvres - Babylone

Built between 1968 and 1970, the Maison des Sciences de l'Homme was the last Parisian project by the French architect, Marcel Lods. The building was designed in collaboration with Henri Beauclair, Paul Deponds and André Malizard, and involved a complex project to incorporate research centres and public institutions working together for human and social sciences. The layout is composed of two main blocks, one facing Boulevard Raspail and the other, Rue du Cherche-Midi. The two blocks are connected by a smaller construction. The building has a steel support structure and features a regular grid facade with transparent glass elements that alternate in a dynamic pattern with folding shutters in perforated aluminium sheet metal. The familiar original facades were not altered during the restoration work, which was limited to the interior. Despite the considerable internal transformation between 2013 and 2017, in collaboration with Michel Rémon, the architect François Chatillon took particular care to respect the facades during the reconstruction project, replacing the aluminium window frames and shutters, as well as the sliding track systems.

© Antoine Mercuso

architects
Marcel Lods / Chatillon
Architectes (restoration)

type
institutional

construction
1968 / 2017

04. Meditation Space UNESCO

32 Avenue de Ségur
75007 Paris

open to the public

www.unesco.org/artcollection

10 > Ségur
6 > Cambronne
6, 8, 10 > La Motte -
Picquet Grenelle

**39, 70, 89, N12,
N13, N61, N62** >
Sèvres - Lecourbe
28, 86 > Duquesne -
Lowendal

Commissioned by UNESCO to commemorate the 50th anniversary of its foundation, the Meditation Space by Tadao Ando was opened on October 25th 1995, and represents the Japanese Pritzker Prize winner's first work in Paris. The strongly symbolic impact of this small circular space, 6 metres in diameter, is enclosed within a cylindrical structure only 30 square metres in area. It is in stark contrast with the vast UNESCO headquarters building designed by Pier Luigi Nervi, Bernard Zehrfuss and Marcel Breuer. It is a memorial monument but also a symbolic celebration of peace. The introspective meditation space is accessed from a walkway leading directly into the main entrance. The walls are built in exposed concrete, and the floor is paved with decontaminated granite from Hiroshima. The simplicity of the composition is enhanced by the carefully calculated and restrained use of light which penetrates from above, enriching the spatial experience of those who visit.

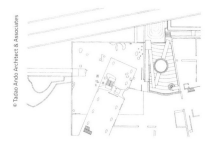

© Tadao Ando Architett & Associates

© Tadao Ando Architect & Associates

architects
Tadao Ando Architect
& Associates

type
monument

construction
1995

05. Australian Embassy

4 Rue Jean Rey
75015 Paris

external viewing only
+33 (0)1 40 59 33 00
consular.paris@dfat.gov.au
france.embassy.gov.au

 6 > Bir-Hakeim

 RER C > Champ
de Mars Tour Eiffel

 30, BUSM6 >
Bir-Hakeim

The Australian Embassy in Paris was the result of the collaboration between the Australian architect Harry Seidler and two consult-
ants, Marcel Breuer and Pier Luigi Nervi. It was
built between 1973 and 1977 in the heart of
Paris only a few hundred metres from the Seine.
The structure is composed of two main curved
buildings skilfully positioned on a triangular plot
formed by the convergence of Rue Jean Rey with
Rue de la Fédération. The buildings, both based
on a quadrant arc design, are set in symmet-
rically specular positions to create a curved S-
shape from the concave and convex facades.
One building contains the Chancellery where
Australia's diplomatic missions to France, OECD
and UNESCO are housed, while the other is a
residential apartment building with 34 apartments for Embassy personnel. The exterior is
imposing and monumental, partly due to the
prefabricated modular concrete containing white
quartz elements that conveys a sense of strict
order to the whole complex.

Architect Harry Seidler & Associates © Penelope Seidler

Harry Seidler © Penelope Seidler

architects
Harry Seidler, Marcel Breuer,
Pier Luigi Nervi

type
institutional

construction
1977

06. Site Tour Eiffel

Champ de Mars,
5 Avenue Anatole France
75007 Paris

partially open to the public

6, 9 > Trocàdero
8 > École Militaire

RER C > Champ
de Mars Tour Eiffel

30, 82 > Tour Eiffel
42, 82 > Champ de
Mars - Suffren
42, 69, 86 > Rapp -
La Bourdonnais

There is no doubt that Gustafson Porter + Bowman's proposal, in preparation for the 2024 Olympic Games, is one of the most far-reaching projects for redesigning public spaces in popular tourist areas in Paris. The project was the subject of an international competition launched by the City of Paris' council in 2018, and includes the redesigning of the 2-kilometre axis connecting the Place du Trocadéro, Palais de Chaillot, Pont d'Iéna, Tour Eiffel, Champ de Mars and the École Militaire. The layout proposed by the landscape architects, who collaborated with Spl Pariseine in their role as project manager, highlights this important thoroughfare composed of distinctive landscape characters, urban corridors, and alternatives to traffic routes, but at the same time, seeks to redefine the iconic area with newly designed green spaces. The proposed layout of the green axis emphasises the symbolic importance and solemnity of this particular area of the city, and aims at reinforcing the perception of the area as an inclusive public space.

© Lorenc Chilabi

architects
Gustafson Porter + Bowman

type
public space

construction
ongoing

07. Musée du Quai Branly

37 Quai Branly
75007 Paris

Tue - Wed, Fri - Sun /
10.30 am - 7.30 pm
Thu / 10.30 am - 10 pm
+33 (0)1 56 61 70 00
billetterie@quaibranly.fr
www.quaibranly.fr

 9 > Alma-Marceau

 REC C > Pont de l'Alma

 42 > Tour Eiffel
80, 92 > Bosquet -
Rapp

Located on the Rive Gauche of the Seine, the Musée du Quai Branly-Jacques Chirac is home to 450,000 artefacts from Asia, Africa, Oceania, and the Americas. Designed by Jean Nouvel, the museum is composed of four buildings: a 200 metre-long centre block containing suspended exhibition galleries; the University block; the "Branly" building, housing the administration offices; and lastly, the "Auvent" that contains the media library. The five storey structure is supported on a network of slender pillars and on the side facing Rue de l'Université, it is filtered by a dense garden of plants from different continents designed by landscape architect, Gilles Clément. The garden forms a transition from the urban to the natural world, leading the visitor into the museum along a ramp that enters the main atrium providing access to the temporary exhibition spaces. An auditorium is located at basement level. A double-height gallery is suspended above the garden: the artefacts on show are classified according to their continents of provenance and are displayed along a flowing circuit that provides visitors with a transversal reading among different cultures. The 25 colourful projecting boxes that animate the facade are designed to create pauses for more detailed analysis of the exhibition circuit inside the building. The museum was designed as a space for ongoing research into the narrative of distant peoples and cultures in a continuous movement of illusions created by the play of changing shapes and colour.

© Ateliers Jean Nouvel

architects
Ateliers Jean Nouvel

type
cultural

construction
2006

08. Palais de Tokyo – extension

13 Avenue du Président Wilson
75116 Paris

Mon - Wed, Fri - Sun /
12 am - 10 pm
Thu / 12 am - 12 pm
+33 (0)1 81 97 35 88

www.palaisdetokyo.com

9 > Iéna
63 > Alma - Marceau

REC C > Pont de l'Alma

63 > Iéna
72 > Musée d'Art
Moderne - Palais
de Tokyo

The Palais de Tokyo was built for the International Exposition of Art and Technology in Modern Life, held in Paris in 1937. It has been used for many different purposes, among which it housed the National Museum of Modern Art, the National Photography Centre, and a large cinema. After many years in disuse, in 1999, the Ministry of Culture decided to restore and renovate the building, and today it is an exhibition space and cultural centre. The Prizker Prize winners, Anne Lacaton and Jean-Philippe Vassal, who won the competition launched to expand and renovate the Palais de Tokyo, were immediately recognised for their spartan approach applied with surgical precision, applying non invasive and sensitive interventions on the original building. The project, which was inaugurated in two separate stages, in 2002 and in 2012, underlined the basic simplicity of the shapes and finishes of the interior, implementing only those minimal transformations necessary to improve accessibility and safety, while providing extensive exhibition and circulation flexibility in the internal spaces.

© Lacaton & Vassal

© Philippe Ruault

architects
Lacaton & Vassal

type
cultural

construction
2014

09. Apple Store Champs-Élysées

**102 Avenue
des Champs-Élysées**
75008 Paris

Mon - Sat / 10 am - 8 pm
Sun / 11 am - 8 pm
+33 (0)1 70 98 09 00

www.apple.com/fr/retail/
champs-elysees

 1 > George V
1, 2, 6 > Charles
de Gaulle - Étoile

 RER A > Charles
de Gaulle - Étoile

 73, N11, N24 >
George V

This project by the international architectural firm Foster + Partners, was created between 2015 and 2018, and is integrated within the historical fabric of one of the French capital's most iconic areas, on the corner of the Champs-Élysées and Rue Washington. The Apple flagship store was incorporated within the pre-existing structure through the redesigning and restoration of the internal spaces of an elegant 19th century apartment building in order to create the store's retail and display spaces. The most radical and visible intervention is the very striking scenographic roof design: the internal courtyard was covered with glass roofing to create an outdoor space for corporate events. The multi-faceted glass roof creates a kaleidoscope effect on the internal facades and the area below, providing an atmosphere dominated by the constantly changing shimmering light on the different facades during the day. Great care was taken to ensure self-producing energy for the project; as well as being the principal design element of the building, the courtyard roofing includes a solar panel system that is able to provide the store's energy supply.

©Nigel Young/ Foster + Partners

architects
Foster + Partners

type
commercial

construction
2018

10. Museé du Louvre (Pyramid and Department of Islamic Arts)

99, Rue de Rivoli /
Quai François Mitterrand
75001 Paris

Mon, Wed, Thu, Sat, Sun /
9 am - 6 pm
Fri / 9 am - 9.45 pm
+33 (0)1 40 20 53 17
info@louvre.fr
www.louvre.fr

 1, 7 > Palais Royal -
Musée du Louvre
14 > Pyramides

 RER C > Musée d'Orsay

 21, 69, 72, N11,
N24 > Palais Royal -
Musée du Louvre
69, 72 > Louvre Rivoli
27, 69, 72, N11,
N24 > Quai François
Mitterrand

The Louvre is the most famous museum in France and among the most renowned in the world. The museum takes its name from the historic building, the Louvre Palace, in which it is housed and which was built in the 12th century. Since its construction, it has been a royal residence, headquarters to different state government bodies, and now, the magnificent museum created at the turn of the 18th and 19th centuries. The complexity linked with any interventions on historic buildings of this symbolic stature is not influenced only by the exceptional level of the project concept itself, but also by the need for sensitivity and expertise in approaching a project of this kind. In the 1980s, despite wide controversy, the then president, François Mitterrand, commissioned the largest renovation program ever carried out in the historic Louvre buildings. The work involved improving the structural access to the museum, while also including a large expansion to cope with the ever-increasing number of visitors. The controversial structure known as the Louvre Pyramid was designed by the architect, Ieoh Ming Pei, and was inaugurated in 1989. It represented a courageous intervention, rejecting any duplication or camouflage, emerging as a contemporary icon. Thanks to its limited but strong architectural elements, the project succeeds in revolutionising not only the perception of the space in front of the museum, but, because of its severe geometry, it has become

architects
Ieoh Ming Pei (Pyramid) /
Rudy Ricciotti, Mario Bellini
(Department of Islamic Arts)

type
cultural

construction
1989 / 2012

99, Rue de Rivoli /
Quai François Mitterrand
75001 Paris

Mon, Wed, Thu, Sat, Sun /
9 am - 6 pm
Fri / 9 am - 9.45 pm
+33 (0)1 40 20 53 17
info@louvre.fr
www.louvre.fr

1, 7 > Palais Royal -
Musée du Louvre
14 > Pyramides

RER C > Musée d'Orsay

21, 69, 72, N11,
N24 > Palais Royal -
Musée du Louvre
69, 72 > Louvre Rivoli
27, 69, 72, N11,
N24 > Quai François
Mitterrand

part of the new collective imaginary linked with
the Louvre. The glass pyramid, the eccentric element of the intervention, acts as a catalyst in
capturing the attention of the visitor, but also
guides the public to the new 46,000 square
metres underground extension, also designed
by Ieoh Ming Pei. The second contemporary
addition to the museum was opened in 2012.
This project provoked less reaction and had less
impact on the overall image of the museum.
The new extension, dedicated to Islamic Arts,
is enclosed within the Visconti courtyard and
covers an area of only 6,800 square metres.
This department, designed by the architects
Mario Bellini and Rudy Ricciotti, is composed
of a low glass structure covered by an undulating anodized aluminium roof which seems
to hover, suspended in the air, while capturing and reflecting the light inside the Neoclassical courtyard.

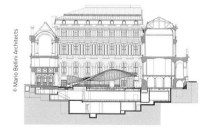

© Mario Bellini Architects

© Raffaele Cipolletta

architects
Ieoh Ming Pei (Pyramid) /
Rudy Ricciotti, Mario Bellini
(Department of Islamic Arts)

type
cultural

construction
1989 / 2012

11. La Samaritaine

9 Rue de la Monnaie
75001 Paris

Mon - Sun / 10 am - 8 pm
+33 (0)1 88 88 60 00
contact.samaritaine@dfs.com
www.lasamaritaine.fr

1 > Louvre - Rivoli
7 > Pont Neuf
4 > Les Halles

RER A, RER B, RER D >
Châtelet - Les Halles

21, 27, 69, 85 > Pont
Neuf - Quai du Louvre
67, 74, 85, N15, N16 >
Rivoli - Pont Neuf

This project, led by the award-winning Japanese architectural firm, SANAA, involved the restoration of a site of great historical and urban importance. It is an area composed of buildings from the 17th century on Rue de l'Arbre Sec and late 19th century buildings, home to the famous Art Nouveau and Art Deco style department store, a short distance from the Louvre. The complex is located in a strategic position and occupies an entire city block with two facades, one in Rue de Rivoli and the other on the Quai du Louvre, facing the Seine. The main focus of the project is centred precisely on the connection between these two important streets that border the area. The "passage de La Samaritaine", is a thoroughfare that will become the nodal point: a new street with commercial activities and stores, winding through the internal spaces and open courtyards of the complex. The approach to the two opposite facades reflects the dual nature of the intervention. The building facing the Seine, designed in 1925 by Henri Sauvage, has been faithfully restored, while the facade on Rue de Rivoli is extremely contemporary, almost liquid and intangible, clad with a membrane of undulating glass that reflects the architecture of the surrounding buildings. A separate element worthy of note is in the historical Rue de la Monnaie, where the building designed by the architect Frantz Jourdain, built between 1905 and 1910 in Art Nouveau style, creates a strong impact because of its exquisite internal and external decoration.

© SANAA

© BERK OZDEMIR / shutterstock.com

architects	type	construction
SANAA	multi-purpose	2021

12. Bourse de Commerce – Pinault Collection

2 Rue de Viarmes
75001 Paris

Mon, Wed, Thu, Sat /
11 am - 7 pm
Fri / 11 am - 9 pm
+33 (0)1 55 04 60 60
info@boursedecommerce.fr
www.boursedecommerce.fr

4 > Les Halles
1 > Louvre - Rivoli

RER A, RER B, RER D >
Châtelet - Les Halles

74, 85, N15, N16 >
Bourse de Commerce,
Louvre Rivoli

This project to restore and reconfigure the Paris Bourse de Commerce as a museum space, is the latest of many transformations the building has sustained over the centuries. The building's current site has undergone a number of interventions, demolitions, and reconstructions since it was first built as the Hôtel de la Reine, home to Catherine de' Medici in the 16th century. The only Medici family traces remaining are the columns on the south-east exterior of the building. The structure assumed its current form in 1889, when it was converted to house the Bourse de Commerce, and in 2021 the building was inaugurated to house the permanent Pinault art collection. The architectural project was the work of the award-winning Japanese firm, Tadao Ando Architect & Associates. The intervention involved the insertion of a pure volume, in the form of a hollow concrete cylinder, within the circular layout of the pre-existant structure. The central space of the cylinder is lit from above through the 19th century glass and steel dome. New museum administration services and elevators/stairs are built round the perimeter of the cylinder.

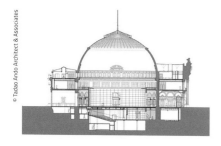

© Tadao Ando Architect & Associates

© Tadao Ando Architect & Associates, NeM / Niney et Marca Architectes, Agence Pierre-Antoine Gatier. Photo by Yuji Ono

architects
Tadao Ando Architect
& Associates

type
cultural

construction
2019

13. Atelier Brâncuși

Place Georges Pompidou
75004 Paris

Mon, Wed - Sun / 2 pm - 6 pm
+33 (0)1 44 78 12 33

www.centrepompidou.fr/fr/
collection/latelier-brancusi

11 > Rambuteau
1 > Hôtel de Ville

RER A, RER B, RER D >
Châtelet - Les Halles

**29, 38, 75, N12, N13,
N14, N23** > Centre
Georges Pompidou

The replica of the Constantin Brâncuși atelier is situated on one side of Place Beaubourg. The reconstruction was assigned to Renzo Piano Building Workshop who designed the famous Centre Pompidou that dominates the opposite side of the square. The reconstruction project was completed in 1997, and is a perfect replica of the original studio. Although the size and volume of the space is limited, the main challenge lay in creating an exhibition space that respected the context and atmosphere of such an intimate and private environment like an artist's studio, so strongly defined by the personality of its author. The aim of completely conserving and preserving the sculptor's spatial relationships inside the studio was even more challenging for the architect, because Brâncuși considered it essential to maintain his personal system of relationships between his various works and with the surrounding space. This included the bases on which his works were displayed, which he considered as works of art in their own right. The Atelier houses all the art works that the Romanian sculptor donated to the French State, including 41 drawings, 2 paintings, and over 1600 glass photographic plates and original prints by the artist. The main body of work consists of 137 sculptures and 87 original bases, arranged in mixed configurations of works which Brâncuși called "mobile groups".

© Michel Denancé

architects
Renzo Piano
Building Workshop

type
cultural

construction
1997

14. Centre Georges Pompidou

Place Georges Pompidou
75004 Paris

Mon, Wed, Fri - Sun /
11 am - 10 pm
Thu / 11 am - 11 pm
+33 (0)1 44 78 12 33

www.centrepompidou.fr

11 > Rambuteau
1, 11 > Hôtel de Ville
1, 4, 7, 11, 14 >
Châtelet

RER A, RER B, RER D >
Châtelet - Les Halles

**29, 38, 47, 75, N12,
N13, N14, N23** >
Centre Georges
Pompidou

In 1971, the French Minister for Culture launched an international architectural competition for the Centre National d'Art et de Culture Georges-Pompidou, also known as Centre Pompidou or more simply, Beaubourg. The two winners, young designers Renzo Piano and Richard Rogers, created what, over time, has become the contemporary icon of Paris, but more importantly, they proposed a new vision for a more flexible and informal type of museum, in strong contrast with the exhibition spaces that had been designed until that time. Opened in 1977, the Centre Pompidou is located at the edge of the Marais, one of the most densely built historic urban areas in the city. The building seems to create a linguistic clash with its surroundings because of its highly technological and "mechanical" impact, and was strategically placed only on one half of the plot assigned for the project. The two architects decided to create a space for social interaction in the area not occupied by the building: the gently sloping public square represents an extension of the museum space, while at the same time, provides a spatial solution to connect the building with the surrounding urban fabric. Since its inauguration, the Centre Pompidou has welcomed over 300 million visitors. Following the work carried out by Renzo Piano between 1997 and 2000 to facilitate public access, a public competition was announced in 2023 to select professionals able to upgrade the museum spaces according to characteristics required by contemporary design standards.

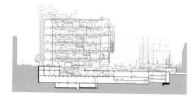

architects
Renzo Piano, Richard Rogers

type
cultural

construction
1977

15. Fondation d'Entreprise Galeries Lafayette

9 Rue du Plâtre
75004 Paris

Mon, Wed, Fri - Sun /
11 am - 7 pm
Thu / 11 am - 9 pm
+ 33 (0)1 42 82 89 98

www.lafayetteanticipations.com

 1, 11 > Hôtel de Ville

 75, 29 > Archives -
Rambuteau
67, 76, 96, N11, N16 >
Hôtel de Ville

The Entreprise Galeries Lafayette Foundation is located in one of the most famous historical areas of Paris: Le Marais. The project involved the restoration and redevelopment of a late 19th century industrial complex to create a new exhibition space, and above all, a centre for innovative cultural productions. Between 2012 and 2018, the international architectural firm, OMA, carried out the delicate work of creating a new function and concept within the pre-existing structure, while respecting listed industrial heritage building restrictions. The project features the insertion of a contemporary element within the internal courtyard of the historic building: it forms a glass tower that fills the courtyard footprint. The flexible infrastructure modifies the rigidity of the former composition with mobile platforms that move up and down to align with the various existing floor levels of the adjacent buildings. This system provides extended modular spaces that can be transformed for a range of different uses.

© OMA

Delfino Sisto Legnani and Marco Cappelletti © OMA

architects	**type**	**construction**
OMA	cultural	2018

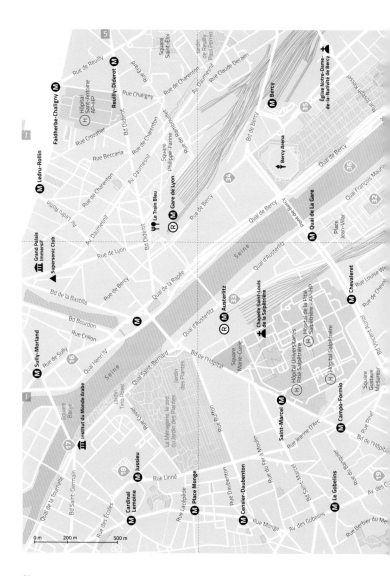

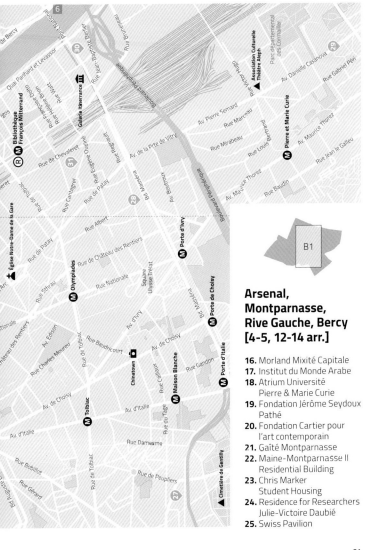

Arsenal, Montparnasse, Rive Gauche, Bercy [4-5, 12-14 arr.]

16. Morland Mixité Capitale
17. Institut du Monde Arabe
18. Atrium Université Pierre & Marie Curie
19. Fondation Jérôme Seydoux Pathé
20. Fondation Cartier pour l'art contemporain
21. Gaîté Montparnasse
22. Maine-Montparnasse II Residential Building
23. Chris Marker Student Housing
24. Residence for Researchers Julie-Victoire Daubié
25. Swiss Pavilion

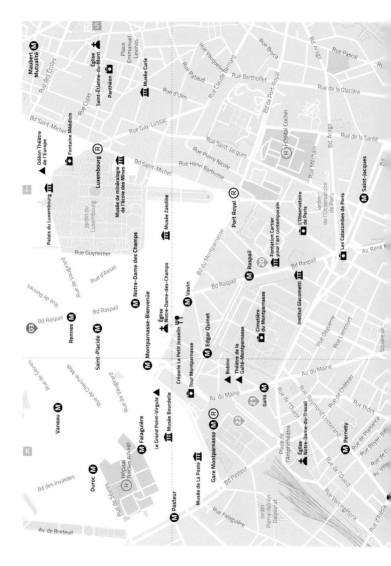

Maubert Mutualité M

Église Saint-Étienne-du-Mont

Place Emmanuel Levinas

Musée Curie

Panthéon

Rue des Écoles

Rue Cujas

Rue Vauquelin

Rue Pratau

Rue Berthollet

Rue Broca

Bd Arago

Rue Pascal

Rue de la Glacière

Rue Claude Bernard

Rue d'Ulm

Bd Saint-Michel

Fontaine Médicis

Odéon Théâtre de l'Europe

Luxembourg R

Rue Gay-Lussac

Bd de Port-Royal

Hôpital Cochin

Rue de la Santé

Palais du Luxembourg

Musée de minéralogie de l'école des Mines

Rue Saint-Jacques

Rue Pierre Nicole

Rue Henri Barbusse

Bd Saint-Michel

Jardin du Luxembourg

Bd Saint-Michel

Port Royal R

Rue Méchain

Bd Arago

H Hôpital

Saint-Jacques M

Musée Zadkine

L'Observatoire de Paris

Fondation Cartier pour l'art contemporain

Jardin de l'Observatoire de Paris

Les Catacombes de Paris

Rue Guynemer

Notre-Dame des Champs

Notre-Dame-des-Champs M

Av. René

Rue d'Assas

Rue de Vaugirard

Rue de Rennes

Raspail M

Vavin M

Bd Raspail

Bd du Montparnasse

Institut Giacometti

Bd Raspail

Rennes 93 Bd Raspail

Montparnasse-Bienvenüe M

Église Notre-Dame-des-Champs

Rue Daguerre

Rue Lalande

Square de

Saint-Placide M

Crêperie Le Petit Josselin

Edgar Quinet M

Cimetière du Montparnasse

Bd Raspail

Rue de Sèvres

Rue de Vaugirard

Tour Montparnasse M

Bobino

Théâtre de la Gaîté-Montparnasse

Av. du Maine

Gaîté M

Rue du Château

Rue Raymond Losserand

Rue de Châtillon

Vaneau M

Rue de Cherche-Midi

Rue de Vaneau

Falguière M

Le Grand Point-Virgule

Musée Bourdelle

Pernety M

Rue de Plaisance

Rue Boyer-Barret

Rue de l'Ouest

Av. Ville

Duroc M

Bd des Invalides

H Hôpital Necker AP-HP

Pasteur M

Musée de La Poste

Gare Montparnasse M R

Place de l'Amphithéâtre

Église Notre-Dame-du-Travail

Rue Vercingétorix

Rue d'Alésia

Av. de Breteuil

Bd Pasteur

Rue Falguière

Jardin Pierre-Adrien Dalpayrat

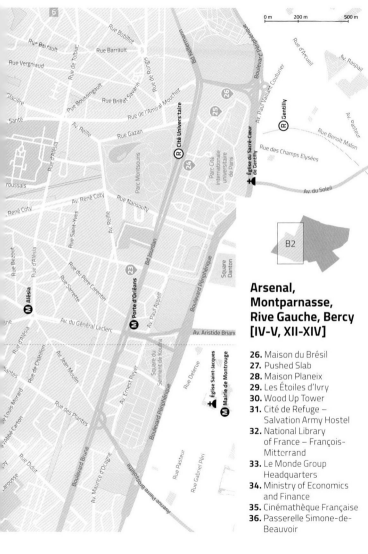

B2

Arsenal, Montparnasse, Rive Gauche, Bercy [IV-V, XII-XIV]

26. Maison du Brésil
27. Pushed Slab
28. Maison Planeix
29. Les Étoiles d'Ivry
30. Wood Up Tower
31. Cité de Refuge –
    Salvation Army Hostel
32. National Library
    of France – François-
    Mittorrand
33. Le Monde Group
    Headquarters
34. Ministry of Economics
    and Finance
35. Cinémathèque Française
36. Passerelle Simone-de-
    Beauvoir

16. Morland Mixité Capitale

17 Boulevard Morland
75004 Paris

open to the public

 7 > Sully - Morland

 72 > Sully - Morland,
Pont de l'Arsenal

This complex originally comprised a 16-storey tower flanked by two 9-storey wings and was completed in about 1960 by the architect, Albert Laprade. In 2014 it was included among the 23 sites in the city selected for the *Réinventer Paris* project in an international competition for redevelopment and extension focussed on economic, social and environmental sustainability. Morland Mixité Capitale won the competition with a project that transformed the ex-Prefecture complex from an enclosed and unapproachable space into a "city within the city". Today, the complex incorporates a wide range of functions: luxury and controlled rent apartments, a hotel, a youth hostel, offices, retail stores, an art gallery, a food market and a child-care centre. Two new buildings create a conciliation between the scale of the existing and neighbouring buildings, inserted harmoniously in the urban fabric. The vaulted arcades of the portico are supported by massive pillars in a formal contrast with the light glazed grid of the upper floors. In the three internal courtyards Michel Desvigne has created a landscaped green space, a miniature forest composed of plant species suited to the specific spaces and climate. The two top storeys house an art installation by Ólafur Elíasson and Sebastian Behmann (Studio Other Spaces) that seems to dematerialise the space thanks to a mirrored ceiling on the 15th floor and a kaleidoscope that blends with the sky on the 16th floor.

© David Chipperfield Architects

architects
David Chipperfield Architects

type
multi-purpose

construction
2022

17. Institut du Monde Arabe

1 Rue des Fossés
Saint-Bernard
75005 Paris

Tue - Fri / 10 am - 6 pm
Sat - Sun / 10 am - 7 pm
+33 (0)1 40 51 38 38

www.imarabe.org/fr

10 > Cardinal Lemoine
7, 10 > Jussieu

63, 89 > Université
Paris VI
67, 75, 87, 89 >
Institut du Monde
Arabe
87 > Pont de la
Tournelle - Cardinal
Lemoine

The Institut du monde arabe, built between 1981 and 1987, is considered one of the signature projects of the French architect, Jean Nouvel, and was his first major project in Paris. The design is based on the juxtaposition of two structures, each with a different form, function and external finish. This dual concept represents the convergence of the two cultures, Western and Eastern. The first building has a regular square footprint and features a complex aluminium and glass facade design. The decorative facade pattern houses a reactive mechanism to allow the passage of natural light into the interior. The design is the most representational aspect of the building and evokes a stylised version of traditional Islamic decoration found in every *mashrabiya*. The second building follows the curving loop of the Seine River, and features a transparent steel and glass facade. This building houses the three floor museum dedicated to Arab and Islamic art and culture throughout history. The Institute integrates various functions combined in a contemporary cultural centre, including a library, a bookshop, a restaurant, a store selling handcrafted products, and an audiovisual room.

© Jean Nouvel (lead architect), Gilbert Lézénès, Pierre Soria, Architecture Studio

© EQRoy / shutterstock.com

architects
Jean Nouvel (lead architect),
Gilbert Lézénès, Pierre Soria,
Architecture Studio

type
cultural

construction
1987

18. Atrium Université Pierre & Marie Curie

4 Place Jussieu
75005 Paris

open to the public

www.sorbonne-universite.fr

11 > Cardinal Lemoine
7, 10 > Jussieu

67, 89 > Jussieu
63, 89 > Cuvier

Located in the quartier du Jardin des Plantes in the 5th arrondissement, the Atrium project was planned to complete the Jussieu Pierre et Marie Curie University Campus designed by the architect Édouard Albert in the 1960s. The expansion, designed by Périphériques Architectes, is based on the pre-existing layout to improve internal circulation. The heavy mass of the concrete building is counterbalanced by the external metal sheet cladding. At ground level, the base of the building is raised with a play of ramps and stairways that connect the street level with the bottom floor of the building. In contrast with the existing rectangular grid layout, an irregular geometrical structure was created in a single block hollowed out to form two patio courtyards: one open to connect with the existing building, and the other, closed to house elevators and stairways. The architects designed this new multi-purpose building as a neutral structure; the facade windows repeat the rythm of those designed by Édouard Albert. The metal skin is composed of ten types of panels perforated with circular holes of different sizes that vary the depth of the facades. The holes also filter the daylight creating a play of light and shadow that changes constantly according to the time of day, and reveals in the evening like a multicolored lighthouse.

© AFJA

architects
Jumeau + Marin + Trottin
/ PÉRIPHÉRIQUES
ARCHITECTES

type
institutional

construction
2006

19. Fondation Jérôme Seydoux Pathé

73 Avenue des Gobelins
75013 Paris

Tue, Fri / 2 pm - 8.30 pm
Wed, Thu / 2 pm - 7 pm
Sat / 11.30 am - 7 pm
+33 (0)1 83 79 18 96
contact@fondationpathe.com
fondation-jeromeseydoux-
pathe.com

 5, 6, 7 > Place d'Italie
7 > Les Gobelins

 **27, 47, 59, 83, N15,
N22** > Banquier
**27, 47, 57, 59, 67,
83, N15, N22, N31,
N139** > Place d'Italie -
Mairie du 13e
57, 67 > Rubens
- École des Arts et
Métiers

Designed in 2014 by Renzo Piano Building Workshop, the new headquarters of the Pathé Foundation is inserted inside an internal space within a dense urban block in the 13th arrondissement in Paris. The structure is built in an area previously occupied by a mid-19th century theatre, converted to house a movie theatre in the 20th century. The new architectural project now houses the archives of the private foundation, the permanent collection and spaces for temporary exhibitions, as well as a 70-seat screening room and the Pathé Foundation's offices. The building is mounted on a curved metal structure attached to adjacent buildings in only a few points. It is roofed with aluminium panels that act as sun shade protection. Viewed from the Avenue des Gobelins, the structure almost seems suspended within the urban space, leaving the expanse free at ground level, where the internal courtyard has been planted with a birch garden.

© RPBW - Renzo Piano Building Workshop Architects

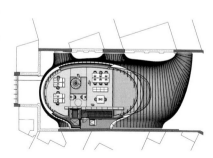

© Michel Denancé, courtesy Fondation Jérôme Seydoux-Pathé

architects
Renzo Piano Building
Workshop

type
cultural

construction
2014

20. Fondation Cartier pour l'art contemporain

261 Boulevard Raspail
75014 Paris

Wed - Sat / 11 am - 8 pm
Tue / 11 am - 10 pm
+33 (0)1 42 18 56 50
boutique.fondation@fondation.
cartier.com
www.fondationcartier.com

 4, 6 > Raspail

 68 > Raspail -
Edgar Quinet
38, N14, N21, N122 >
Denfert-Rochereau –
Arago

The headquarters of the Fondation Cartier pour l'art contemporain has been located in Boulevard Raspail in the Montparnasse quarter since 1994. It was designed by the French architect, Jean Nouvel, in 1994, and till now, housed the famous French Cartier art collection. The building will soon be converted to an office block as the Foundation recently announced it would be transferring its exhibition space to the historic Louvre des Antiquaires building. The current building is surrounded by a woodland garden with over 240 plant and wild flower species and was famous for a two hundred year old cedar of Lebanon that had to be cut down in 2020. The building's glass facades disappear amidst the greenery, concealing the conceptual size of the building. The interaction between the indoor and outdoor spaces was a deliberate design concept and the vast glazed surfaces intersected by the steel lattice structure blur the building's boundaries. In the words of the architect: "in a poetic blend of illusion and uncertainty".

© Jean Nouvel, Emmanuel Cattani & Associés

© Philippe Ruault

architects
Jean Nouvel, Emmanuel
Cattani & Associés

type
cultural

construction
1994

21. Gaîté Montparnasse

68/80 Avenue du Maine
75014 Paris

Mon - Sat / 10 am - 8 pm
+33 (0)1 43 27 99 69

www.lesateliersgaite.com

13 > Gaîté
6 > Edgar Quinet

**N, TGV, TGV INOUI,
TER, TER23 OUIGO** >
Gare Montparnasse

59, 88, N63, N66 >
Jean Zay - Maine
58, 92 > Gaîté
59, 88, 91 > Place
de La Catalogne

This intervention, completed in 2022 by the Dutch architectural firm MVRDV, was designed to rationalise and transform a city block previously occupied by a multi-purpose urban complex with a range of activities and services, including a hotel, a shopping centre, office buildings, and a library. The new solutions proposed by the architects were aimed at making the urban block more easily accessible to the public with significant changes in the relationship between the building and the surrounding urban fabric, while at the same time providing extra residential space by including social housing and a kindergarten. The project was based on a sensitive and sustainable approach aimed at preserving many of the existing structural elements while the main interventions focussed on changing the spatial concept and overall public image of the entire urban block.

© MVRDV

© Ossip van Duivenbode

architects
MVRDV

type
multi-purpose building

construction
2022

22. Maine-Montparnasse II Residential Building

Rue du Commandant Mouchotte
75015 Paris

external viewing only

 14 > Gaîté
6 > Edgar Quinet

 N, TGV, TGV INOUI, TER, TER23 OUIGO >
Gare Montparnasse

 59, 88, N63, N66 >
Jean Zay - Maine
58, 92 > Gaîté
59, 88, 91 > Place
de La Catalogne

 T3a > Avenue
de France

The Maine-Montparnasse II residential building, designed by Jean Dubuisson between 1962 and 1966, is one of the main components in the panorama of the much larger Maine-Montparnasse urban planning project. The operation also included the well-known Tour Montparnasse (1969-73) designed by the architects Eugène Beaudouin, Urbain Cassan, and Louis Hoym de Marien, the Sheraton Hotel (1971-74) by architect Pierre Dufau, and the Maine-Montparnasse I and Maine-Montparnasse II apartment blocks, both designed by Dubuisson. Maine-Montparnasse II is located in Rue du Commandant René Mouchotte that flanks the Jardin Atlantique and counterbalances the Maine-Montparnasse I block that borders the park on the opposite side. The building is exceptional for its size: 88,000 square metres divided into 18 floors, with 750 housing units of varying types, from studio flats to duplex apartments. The facade features a regular frame structure with a grid-like pattern harmoniously repeated along the entire building. The facades are not load-bearing, and are completely glazed to provide maximum natural light.

architects
Jean Dubuisson

type
residential

construction
1966

23. Chris Marker Student Housing

154 Rue de la Tombe Issoire
75014 Paris

external viewing only
+ 33 (0) 1 40 51 35 05

 4 > Porte d'Orléans

 RER B > Cité
Universitaire

 88, 216, Orlybus >
Montsouris -
Tombe Issoire
**Traverse Bièvres
Montsouris** >
Place Jules Henaffe

This project, created between 2007 and 2018 by the French architects Éric Lapierre, Laurent Esmilaire and Tristan Chadney (now Experience), is exceptional for its size and spatial concept. 100 metres long and 31 metres high, it is situated in the 14th arrondissement and the design has managed to convey the internal complexity of the project with a sharp clean urban image. The large number of stairways and elevators, plus the spaces between each floor – corridors, passageways, diagonal elevators, and vertical companionways, such as the internal stairs and the enormous external staircase – can be interpreted as the driving force that generates the public space. In this way, new standards were defined to create greater communication between the individual housing units and communal spaces in a student residence that is part of a wider urban planning scheme; the residence is part of a multi-purpose building constructed over a RATP bus depot and garage on ground level. The large range of internal passages can also be identified through the design of the facades, while on the side of the building facing the street, a strong diagonal line leads to multiple public spaces on the different floors. The internal facade is dominated by a monumental terraced structure connected to the communal spaces.

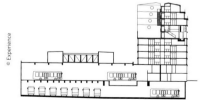

© Experience

©Filip Dujardin

architects
Experience

type
multi-purpose

construction
2018

24. Residence for Researchers Julie-Victoire Daubié

27F Boulevard Jourdan
75014 Paris

external viewing only
+33 (0) 1 43 13 55 00

www.ciup.fr/maisons/
residence-julie-victoire-daubie

RER B > Cité Universitaire

88 > Jourdan - Montsouris

T3a > Montsouris

Located on the southern edge of the Cités Universitaire's vast park in Paris, this residence for young researchers, designed by the architecture office BRUTHER, makes a strong architectural statement in the urban fabric despite the simplicity of its materials and design. Unencumbered on its four sides, the residence is immediately identifiable as a "split and raised" cube, the organization of which is easily readable in its section. Above the reception areas located in the semi-buried garden level, the first floor of the apartments is 2.90 metres above the ground level of the Cité Universitaire. The 106 apartments (1-bed to 3-beds) are distributed over seven levels. The typological organization of the plan resides in three parallel strips oriented on a north-south line: two are dedicated to housing units and between them, a hollow strip accommodates all circulation cores. Far from simple functionalism, the triangular staircase and the elevator are assertive, autonomous plastic volumes. On the eighth and last floor, the circulation area widens to form a large collective terrace, protected by transparent railings, while the top of the "East strip" houses a fitness room with a view of the city. In a way, it becomes possible to jog along the périphérique ring road. These common facilities affirm the collective dimension of the building, as well as its spectacular relationship with its environment.

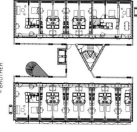

© BRUTHER

architects
BRUTHER

type
residential

construction
2017

25. Swiss Pavilion

7K Boulevard Jourdan
75014 Paris

Mon - Sun / 10 am - 12 pm,
2 pm - 5 pm
+33 (0)1 44 16 10 16

www.fondationsuisse.fr

 RER B > Cité
Universitaire

 21, 216 > Stade
Charlety - Porte
de Gentilly
125 > Gentilly RER

 T3a > Stade Charléty -
Porte de Gentilly, Cité
Universitaire

Located in the Cité Internationale Universitaire in the 14th arrondissement, the Swiss Pavilion is a residence for Swiss students designed between 1931 and 1933 by Le Corbusier and Pierre Jeanneret. The building design is based on the juxtaposition of three different elements, each one identifiable for its form and function: the main block houses the students' rooms, a lower entrance building contains all the communal spaces on the ground floor, while a third block houses the stairs and elevators. The architectural design was created completely in line with Le Corbusier's concept of modern architecture and is one of his first experiments for a collective housing structure. The building is raised from ground level on pillars, leaving abundant space for easy circulation between public spaces at ground level. The layout and the facade have plain simple lines and feature ribbon windows that dominate the main facade. The entire residential block is surmounted with a roof-terrace accessible from the top floor. The interior design, created in collaboration with Charlotte Perriand, features 42 mini-apartments: each is minimal in size (6×2,8 m) but able to incorporate all elements necessary for daily habitation.

© Denis Esakov

architects
Le Corbusier, Pierre Jeanneret

type
residential

construction
1931

26. Maison du Brésil

7L Boulevard Jourdan
75014 Paris

Mon - Fri / 10 am - 1 pm,
2 pm - 6 pm
+33 (0)1 83 94 40 04
maisondubresil@
maisondubresil.org
www.maisondubresil.org

RER B > Cité
Universitaire

21, 216 > Stade
Charléty - Porte
de Gentilly
125 > Gentilly RER

T3a > Stade Charléty -
Porte de Gentilly,
Cité Universitaire

The Maison du Brésil is located in the Cité Inter-nationale Universitaire of Paris, a short distance from the Swiss Pavilion, also designed by Le Corbusier, and was inaugurated in 1959. For this project, the father of Modern European Architecture worked in collaboration with the well-known Brazilian architect and urban plan-ning designer, Lúcio Costa, who later removed his name from the project. In this project, Le Corbusier applied a more mature and Brutal-ist concept, changing some of the lessons he learned when designing his more renowned Unité d'habitation, but working with smaller pro-portions than those he used on his Marseilles project. Once again, the main block is built in exposed concrete, raised above the ground on concrete pilotis. The west facade has a distinc-tive feature as each unit has a covered balcony, painted internally in alternating bright colours, some inspired by the Brazilian flag. The colours are repeated to accentuate certain internal fea-tures such as columns, doors and internal walls.

© Denis Esakov

architects
Le Corbusier, Lúcio Costa

type
institutional

construction
1957

27. Pushed Slab

10 Rue Brillat-Savarin
75013 Paris

external viewing only

7 > Maison Blanche,
Porte d'Italie

**Traverse Bièvres
Montsouris** >
Küss, Peupliers

T3a > Poterne
des Peupliers

This complex was completed in 2014 by the internationally famous architects, MVRDV, on a former railway embankment site. It covers an area of 4,000 square metres and is set between two different urban contexts: dense city fabric to the north, and the more expanded boulevards to the south. This city office block takes its name from the concept behind its composition. The floor slabs were dynamically extruded to form multiple terrace spaces, both outdoors and under cover in an irregular composition to create diversified perspectives. Pushed Slab is the first element in a far greater urban redevelopment plan aimed at transforming the 13th arrondissement in Paris into a so-called Green District. The building has incorporated a large number of energy efficient strategies and technologies including 264 solar panels and 22 solar thermal collectors. Special attention has been paid to water disposal systems and thermal insulation. The facade of the building has adopted sustainable solutions with wooden cladding certified by the Forest Stewardship Council.

© MVRDV

© Philippe Ruault

architects
MVRDV

type
offices

construction
2014

28. Maison Planeix

24bis Boulevard Masséna
75013 Paris

external viewing only

7 > Porte d'Ivry
14 > Olympiades

27 > Masséna -
Darmesteter
N31, 27 >
Porte de Vitry
N31 > Château
des Rentiers

T3a > Porte d'Ivry,
Maryse Bastié

Maison Planeix was commissioned by the painter and sculptor Antonin Planeix in 1924. It is an urban residential building divided into various housing units overlooking Boulevard Masséna, not far from the Brutalist fire station designed by Jean Willerval in 1971. According to the instructions of their client, Le Corbusier and Pierre Jeanneret planned two independent apartments on the ground floor, infringing one of Le Corbusier's fundamental standards, generally based on an open unrestricted ground floor supported on pilotis. The first floor houses the sculptor's apartment, while the owner's art studio occupies the second floor. Lastly, an element that is often part of Le Corbusier's designs: the entire building is surmounted by a roof-terrace with views over the rear garden. Like many of the architect's projects from the 1920s, the design features very plain lines based on a composition of simple shapes: the only detail that interrupts the regular lines of the facade is a projecting element that acts as a bow-window for the first floor, providing a support for the overhanging terrace on the second floor.

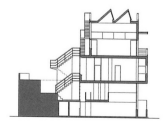

architects
Le Corbusier

type
residential

construction
1928

29. Les Étoiles d'Ivry

79-81 Avenue
Danielle Casanova
94200 Ivry-sur-Seine

external viewing only

 7 > Mairie D'Ivry

 RER C > Ivry-sur-Seine

 132, N133 >
Ivry sur Seine
Noctilien - Voltaire
125, 323 > Hôtel
de Ville d'Ivry

Located in the commune of Ivry-sur-Seine, south-east of Paris, with its strong dynamic energy the Étoiles d'Ivry complex embodies some of the most interesting experiments in the residential architecture of the 1960s and 1970s. Just outside the Boulevard Périphérique ring road, the area where the complex was built became the object of increasing interest just after the war in answer to the growing demand for housing in major cities. Named after figures in the French Resistance, the buildings, designed by architects Renée Gailhoustet and Jean Renaudie between 1970 and 1975, were part of a wider development scheme supervised by Gailhoustet. The aim of the architects was to renovate and rebuild the centre of Ivry-sur-Seine with a series of exceptional building designs that would break up the monotonous repetitive style of the large blocks and towers of the existing social housing. The complex composition and layout makes this intervention one of the most original social housing projects of the last century. The designers were able to harmoniously integrate a range of functions: public spaces, schools, shops, services, offices and housing, a concept similar to those within an urban organism. Externally, the structures are powerfully Brutalist, but their massive effect is constantly interrupted by unusual sculptural shapes that give the complex a fragmented image.

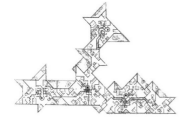

architects
Renée Gailhoustet,
Jean Renaudie

type
residential

construction
1974

30. Wood Up Tower

25 Quai d'Ivry
75013 Paris

external viewing only

 14 > Bibliothèque
François-Mitterrand

 RER C > Bibliothèque
François Mitterrand

 62 > Porte de France
25, 325 > Watt

 T3a > Avenue
de France

Located on the banks of the Seine near the Boulevard Périphérique ring road, this 50 metre tower project is built in the Masséna-Bruneseau area of the 13th arrondissement in Paris. It is a residential building, and includes communal spaces and collective functions, open to the city; the 17 storey building has a structure built entirely in wood. The material clearly plays the leading role in the building's design, where the project shows all the possible applications from the exoskeleton to the cladding. The technical challenge, especially the structural performance, had a strong influence on space layout choices. This represented the starting point for the LAN design in their experiment to construct a tower with a material that was unconventional for this kind of building. The spacious ground floor with its high ceilings now forms a socialising space and a filter with the urban surroundings.

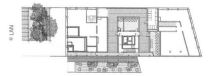

© LAN

architects	type	construction
LAN	multi-purpose	2024

31. Cité de Refuge – Salvation Army Hostel

37 Rue du Cantagrel
75013 Paris

external viewing only
+33 (0) 1 43 62 25 00

www.armeedusalut.fr

 14 > Bibliothèque
François Mitterrand

 RER C > Bibliothèque
François Mitterrand

 27, 132, N31 > Oudiné
27, 132 > Regnault

 T3a > Maryse Bastie,
Avenue de France

Built between 1929 and 1933 by Le Corbusier and Pierre Jeanneret in the 13th arrondissement in Paris, this building was designed as a very clear and ambitious project from the very beginning. It needed to satisfy the priorities of the Salvation Army as well as offering a refuge for the most disadvantaged. The accommodation capacity was about 500 beds in dormitories or small single rooms, supported by a system of services for the residents aimed at creating a veritable city-refuge. The gamble taken by the architects with this project was the creation of an airtight facade on the south-facing side, which required forced ventilation for the internal spaces with totally glazed curtain walls, but without windows that could be opened. In fact, the south facade on Rue Cantagrel was the object of several modifications that had to be made to the building. The first was decided by the architects themselves between 1948 and 1950 to repair damage caused by bombing during the war, and to correct the absence of thermal comfort on the southern side with the addition of a lightweight raw concrete brise-soleil.

architects
Le Corbusier, Pierre Jeanneret

type
institutional

construction
1933

32. National Library of France – François-Mitterrand

Quai François Mauriac
75706 Paris

Mon / 2 pm - 8 pm
Tue - Sat / 9 am - 8 pm
Sun / 1 pm - 7 pm
+33 (0)1 53 79 59 59

www.bnf.fr/en/francois-mitterrand

 14 > Bibliothèque François Mitterrand
6 > Quai de la Gare

 RER C > Bibliothèque François Mitterrand

 89, 325 > Bibliothèque Nationale de France
71, 89, 325 > Émile Durkheim
25, 64, 325, 71 > Pont de Tolbiac

The National Library of France was one of the last great Parisian projects planned by President François Mitterrand. Inaugurated in 1995, it offers the city a genuine contemporary monument rising on the banks of the Seine. Its bijective relationship with the urban space, and its design, which blends the constructed space with the open public space, makes the building a cardinal element in this urban area. Four towers mark the boundaries of the intervention. Each tower has a name: Tour des temps, Tour des lois, Tour des nombres and Tour des lettres (Time, Law, Numbers, Literature). The Library layout is arranged within an enclosure, defined by the four corner towers, and a large public space on an urban scale surrounds a sunken garden. An imposing wooden stairway leads visitors from the banks of the Seine up to the raised public space that connects the four towers. The Library contains a seemingly infinite sequence of archives and reference collections. The building can accommodate about 3,600 visitors in the reading rooms, office spaces, galleries and conference rooms.

© Dominique Perrault architecte_ Adagp

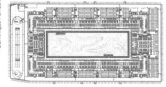

© Georges Fessy _ Dominique Perrault Architecte _ Adagp

architects
Dominique Perrault

type
cultural

construction
1995

33. Le Monde Group Headquarters

**69 Avenue Pierre
Mendès-France**
75013 Paris

external viewing only
+33 (0)1 57 28 20 00

The newly completed French Le Monde Group Headquarters in Avenue Pierre-Mendès-France in the 13th arrondissement in Paris, was opened in 2020. The main structure, designed by the international architectural firm, Snøhetta, rises between the adjacent Austerlitz railway line on one side, and the large avenue on the other, and was designed to connect and integrate with both areas. Le Monde building forms a vast bridging arch over a public plaza at ground level which connects the railway station area with Avenue Pierre-Mendès-France. The facades of the building are clad with over 20,000 glass elements, each one representing a distinct pixel ranging from transparent to opaque according to its position, to permit maximum daylight penetration into the internal spaces within the building.

 5, 10 > Gare
d'Austerlitz
6 > Quai de la Gare,
Chevaleret

 RER C > Gare
d'Austerlitz

 C, N131, N133 >
Paris Austerlitz
61, 89, 215 >
Cité de La Mode
et du Design
**24, 57, 61, 63, 89,
N131, N133** >
Gare d'Austerlitz

© Snøhetta

architects
Snøhetta, SRA Architectes

type
offices, public space

construction
2020

34. Ministry of Economics and Finance

139 Rue de Bercy
75012 Paris

external viewing only
+33 (0)1 40 04 04 04

www.economie.gouv.fr

6, 14 > Bercy
1, 14 > Gare
de Paris Lyon

RER A, RER D >
Gare de Lyon

**24, 77, 87, N32, N35,
N130** > Ministère
de l'Economie et
des Finances –
Gare de Lyon
**24, 77, 87, N32,
N35** > Gare de Lyon -
Maison de La RATP
71, 215 > Bercy -
Arena

Built between 1982 and 1989, the new French Ministry of Finance occupies five buildings: Colbert, Vauban and Necker (designed by architects Paul Chemetov and Borja Huidobro), and the remaining two buildings, Sully and Turgot, which were the work of architects Louis Arretche and Roman Karasinski. The main and most iconic structure, Colbert, is built like a multi-span bridge or viaduct that stretches for a length of over 300 metres. Situated perpendicular to the Seine, it spans the railway line to reach the river, where it is anchored in the river bed. The immense size and mass of the building recalls ancient classical structures with its monumental proportions and two 70 metre spans, connected by smaller sized arches. The interior of the building is designed as a flexible organism, and for this reason, it was constructed with a modular layout composed of basic elements measuring 90×90 cm: the height of the office spaces is equal to three times the module size, while the distance from one flooring to another is four times the size.

architects
Paul Chemetov, Borja
Huidobro, Louis Arretche,
Roman Karasinski

type
institutional

construction
1986

35. Cinémathèque Française

51 Rue de Bercy
75012 Paris

Mon, Wed - Fri / 12 pm - 7 pm
Sat - Sun / 11 am - 7 pm
+33 (0)1 71 19 33 33

www.cinematheque.fr

6, 14 > Bercy
14 > Cour Saint-Émilion

24, N32 >
Bercy - Aréna
**24, 64, BUSM14,
N32** > Dijon –
Lachambeaudie –
Cour Saint-Émilion

This building is the result of a composition made up of several solid blocks of varying shapes and sizes that look outwards with strictly regular window openings on the frontages of Rue de Bercy and Rue Jean Renoir; the windows almost seem to replicate traditional Parisian facades in another fashion, imposed with rigorous precision. The architect's plan to model this architectural work as a piece of sculpture made up of a juxtaposition of squared blocks and rounded solids, was naturally limited by dimensional restrictions which probably influenced its evolution. The construction site boundary was strictly circumscribed on two sides, but opened up facing the park, permitting greater freedom for structure and surface development. The three materials used for construction are those traditionally used in Paris: glass, zinc, and Saint-Maximin limestone, the same as that used for the construction of Palais Royal and many other Parisian buildings. With these materials, Frank Gehry proposed a balance between tradition and innovation, creating a distinctive landmark for the neighbourhood. Between 1994 and 1996, the building was the headquarters of the American Center, but remained empty for the next nine years before becoming home to the Cinémathèque Française in 2003. The interior was remodeled by Atelier de l'île, winner of a public competition launched in 1999. It now includes four projection rooms, a museum, a space for temporary exhibitions, a media library, teaching workshops, a restaurant and logistics facilities.

architects
Frank Gehry / Atelier de l'île

type
cultural

construction
1994 / 2003

36. Passerelle Simone-de-Beauvoir

**Passerelle
Simone-de-Beauvoir**
75012 Paris

open to the public

 6, 14 > Bercy
6 > Quai de la Gare

 Intercités > Bercy

 89, 325 > Bibliothèque
Nationale de France
24, N32 > Bercy -
Arena

Built between 2004 and 2006, the new bridge on the Seine, dedicated to the feminist writer and philosopher Simone de Beauvoir, is an urban structure designed exclusively for pedestrian use. The 300 metre-long bridge connects the two banks of the Seine, linking the Parc de Bercy in the 12th arrondissement with the François-Mitterrand Library in the 13th. The competition launched in 1998 was won by the architectural firm Dietmar Feichtinger, who designed the bridge with a fluid organic form. The two main lines of the project are based on a development in opposite directions to create two arches, one concave and one convex, that meet in the central point of the bridge. Despite the long distance between the two banks, the bridge is composed of a single span without intermediate support piers, leaving the main central river flow unrestricted, and reducing the visual impact of the structure.

© Dietmar Feichtinger Architects

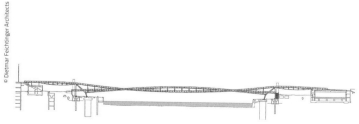

architects
Dietmar Feichtinger
Architects

type
infrastructure

construction
2006

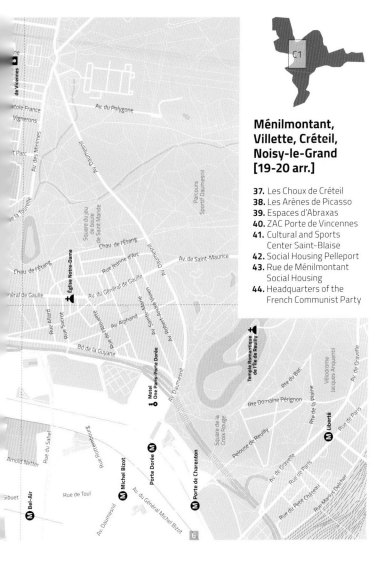

Ménilmontant, Villette, Créteil, Noisy-le-Grand [19-20 arr.]

37. Les Choux de Créteil
38. Les Arènes de Picasso
39. Espaces d'Abraxas
40. ZAC Porte de Vincennes
41. Cultural and Sports Center Saint-Blaise
42. Social Housing Pelleport
43. Rue de Ménilmontant Social Housing
44. Headquarters of the French Communist Party

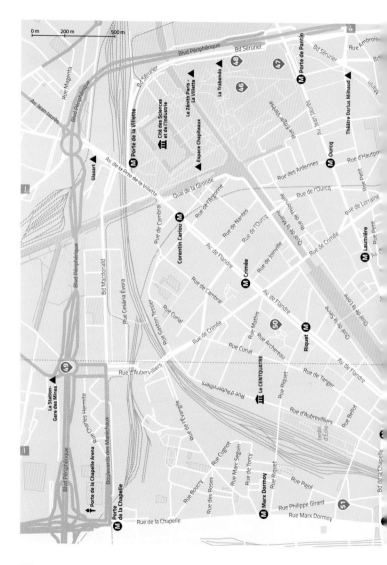

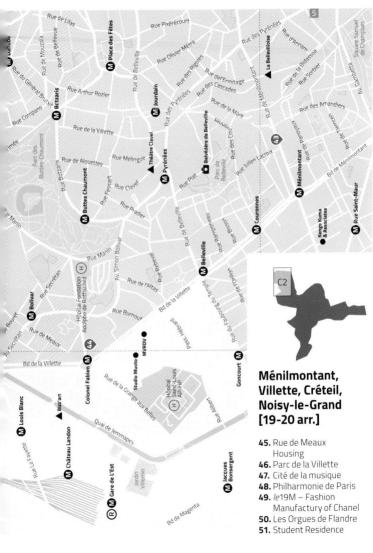

C2

Ménilmontant, Villette, Créteil, Noisy-le-Grand [19-20 arr.]

45. Rue de Meaux Housing
46. Parc de la Villette
47. Cité de la musique
48. Philharmonie de Paris
49. *le*19M – Fashion Manufactury of Chanel
50. Les Orgues de Flandre
51. Student Residence

37. Les Choux de Créteil

2 Boulevard Pablo Picasso
94000 Créteil

external viewing only

RER A > Noisy-le-
Grand Mont d'Est train
station

N71, Tvm > Préfecture
du Val-de-Marne
181, 281 > Université

Les Choux de Créteil architectural project, built between 1969 and 1974 in the Val-de-Marne district, is part of a much wider urban planning scheme for the area, called *Nouveau Créteil*. As well as the vast projects for residential buildings, the scheme also envisaged a series of administrative structures: prefecture, law court, hospital, archives, and city council building approved for the recent creation of the Val-de-Marne Department, which was established in 1968. Les Choux, (literally "cabbages") because of the leaf-shape of their projecting curved balconies, are a group of 11 cylindrical social housing buildings designed by the architect Gérard Grandval. The 11 towers were designed with a circular layout, and the dominating feature of the facades is the concrete balconies in curved sculptural form that cover the buildings on every floor.

architects
Gérard Grandval

type
residential

construction
1974

38. Les Arènes de Picasso

6 Place Pablo Picasso
93160 Noisy-le-Grand

external viewing only

RER A > Gare de Noisy-le-Grand - Mont d'Est

206, 310, E, N34 > Noisy-le-Grand - Mont d'Est RER

Designed by the Spanish architect Manuel Núñez Yanowsky, who studied under Bofill, the Arènes de Picasso residential complex was inaugurated in Noisy-le-Grand In 1985. The zone lies on the perimeter of the new Marne-la-Vallée city development, and was part of the urban planning scheme launched in the 1960s in answer to the Parisian housing crisis following the Second World War. The complex designed by Yanowsky sits alongside a project designed by Bofill, a short distance away, in a dialogue with Les Espaces d'Abraxas with a similar monumental, majestic scale and experimental design. The complex houses 540 social housing units grouped around a central courtyard-arena and features two vast cylinders inserted into a lower rectangular structure that circumscribes the internal space. The two 16 storey cylindrical structures that frame the two ends of the project have assumed such an iconic identity in the local imaginary, that the residents have nicknamed the project "the camemberts".

© Arthur Weidmann CC BY-SA 4.0

architects
Manuel Núñez Yanowsky

type
residential

construction
1985

39. Espaces d'Abraxas

Rue du Clos des Aulnes
93160 Noisy-le-Grand

external viewing only

RER A > Gare de Noisy-
le-Grand - Mont d'Est

120 > Lycée
International
206, 207, 306, 310 >
Cimetière de Noisy-
le-Grand

Composed of 600 housing units, Les Espaces d'Abraxas is an important residential project inaugurated in 1983 in the Mont d'Est quarter of Noisy-le-Grand in the Seine-Saint-Denis Department. The project adopts many elements from classical architecture resulting in an austere but harmonious appearance. The Spanish architect, Ricardo Bofill, used a repertoire of columns, pediments, grooved half-pilasters and monumental proportions. The complex is composed of three main buildings: the 18 storey "Palace" inspired by Neoclassical style that contrasts with the "Theatre", a semi-circular block which recalls ancient amphitheatres. Between the two is the "Arch" in the centre of the configuration. If, on one hand, the exceptional architectural style of the project has gained global fame, (it has been featured as a backdrop for Hollywood and TV films), on the other, only a few years after its inauguration, the social and residential utopia was rapidly reduced to an environment that was unsafe, accelerating its architectural decline. It was only in 2018 that a cultural project was launched for the restoration of the project, supervised by the architect Bofill himself.

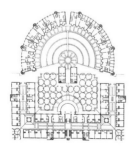

architects
Ricardo Bofill Taller
de Arquitectura

type
residential

construction
1983

40. ZAC Porte de Vincennes

Rue Cristino Garcia
75020 Paris

open to the public

1 > Porte de Vincennes
9 > Porte de Montreuil

86, 215, 351, N11,
Traverse Charonne >
Porte de Vincennes
Traverse Charonne >
Hilsz - Lagny, Schubert
- Paganini

T3a, T3b > Porte
de Vincennes
T3b > Porte
de Montreuil

This park was created on the border between the 12th and 20th arrondissements, next to Porte de Vincennes. The park is located at the intersection of the Boulevard Périphérique, the external ring road around Paris, and the radial road that leads towards the consolidated city centre. The intervention by Topotek 1 landscape architects was not limited to upgrading and renovating the existing public space, with planting and the creation of new pathways. The architects decided to define more appropriate spaces for the community. The core area of the park was equipped with a 50 metre, red metal structure, designed as an attraction for children to play on and for physical exercise for adults. The aim was to create a symbolic element to encourage social interaction in the neighbourhood. The green zone, parallel to the central square, is designed to provide a sound barrier against heavy traffic, as well as a visual and spatial protection for the park.

© Topotek 1

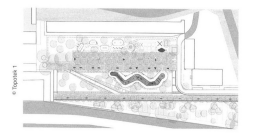

architects
Topotek 1

type
public space

construction
2020

41. Cultural and Sports Center Saint-Blaise

15 Rue Mouraud
75020 Paris

Mon / 2 pm - 10 pm
Tue - Fri / 10 am - 10 pm
Sat / 10 am - 7 pm

 9 > Porte de Montreuil

 Traverse charonne >
Orteaux - Maraichers
57 > Porte de Montreuil

 T3b > Porte
de Montreuil

The building, designed by the architecture office BRUTHER, is situated in the Saint-Blaise district, one of the densest in Europe. The project plot is surrounded by high buildings from the 1980s that form an enclave around it. In this context, the void is rare and precious, so that in order to establish itself in this void while preserving it, the building opts for compactness and leaving free its four faces, it extends vertically up to 16.88 metres, thus saving the ground. The facades feature different transparent and opaque sections according to the type of activities performed inside the building. The choice of these materials is aimed at reinforcing the project's community objective by strengthening relationships with the neighbourhood. One of the core elements of the project design is to create an inviting atmosphere for the surrounding urban environment: several sections of the facades are transparent so that the structural elements are visible from the exterior showing the plain unadorned treatment of the internal areas. The spaces within the new building have been designed to be highly flexible to provide wider variety for the needs of the community as well as the possibility of modification and refurbishment for different uses in the future.

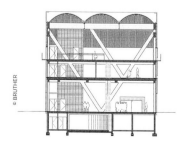

© BRUTHER

BRUTHER © Julien Hourcade

architects
BRUTHER

type
multi-purpose

construction
2015

42. Social Housing Pelleport

133-135 Rue Pelleport
75020 Paris

external viewing only

 11 > Télégraphe

 60 > Borrego

This social housing project, completed by the architectural firm BRUTHER in 2017, is located on an irregularly shaped site in the 20th arrondissement in the north-east of Paris. The area has undergone rapid expansion in recent years and this project caters for 25 social housing units of different sizes and styles. In this project, the fundamental architectural style for which the architects are recognised is expressed through the vast sections of aluminium framed glazing across the whole facade. The glazed sections are inserted into the concrete structure to create a very light visual effect. Although this is a single building, it is composed of two different constructions: the facades are built along two converging streets which enclose the entire plot: Rue Pelleport and Rue des Pavillons. The facade along Rue Pelleport is dynamic and transparent, featuring enclosed glazed winter gardens on the upper floors, while the ground floor houses retail stores at street level. In Rue des Pavillons, the building has one less floor because of the street slope, and the facade has a more regular design. Full height, adjustable internal curtains provide shade from the balconies and add variety through the different curtain colours that can be glimpsed from the exterior. The colour scheme for the balcony facade curtains was suggested by the architects and was adopted by most of the residents.

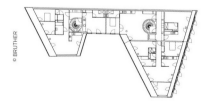

© BRUTHER

BRUTHER · Maxine Delvaux

architects
BRUTHER

type
residential, commercial

construction
2017

43. Rue de Ménilmontant Social Housing

Rue de Ménilmontant
75021 Paris

external viewing only

 2 > Ménilmontant

 96 > Julien Lacroix

This social housing project was one of the most iconic interventions in Paris in the 1980s. It is situated in Ménilmontant, which was originally a village, and later a suburb of the French capital, annexed with the city only in 1860 by Baron Haussmann. Today it is integrated within the 20th arrondissement. Built in 1986, the building sits within a complex and varied urban fabric, but without sacrificing any of its specific identity. On the street frontage, the facade follows the alignment of the surrounding buildings, while on the internal courtyard side, slight curves, recesses, alternating planes and voids provide an independent movement, especially in the corner structure. The courtyard is also influenced by the complex architecture with its internal concave and convex facades that create an irregular shape. The small ceramic tile cladding generates a light coloured integral effect on the building's facades.

© Giulia Cerretani

architects
Henri Gaudin, Isabelle Marin

type
residential

construction
1986

44. Headquarters of the French Communist Party

2 Place du Colonel Fabien
75019 Paris

external viewing only
+33 (0)1 44 83 85 15
bienvenue@paris.pcf.fr
paris.pcf.fr

 2 > Colonel Fabien

 46, 75, BUSM2 >
Colonel Fabien

Located near the Parc des Buttes Chaumont, the headquarters of the French Communist Party designed by Oscar Niemeyer overlooks the Place du Colonel Fabien and is set in the typically 19th century fabric of Belleville, a former working class area of Paris. Opened in 1972 and registered as a historical monument in 2007, the exterior of the so-called "Home of the Communist Party" is composed of two apparently distinct elements that form the complex. Above ground are the admirable continuous facades designed by French architect Jean Prouvé and executed with extreme technical precision, but the building reveals its complexity in the floors below ground that form and connect the two structures visible from the exterior. The first building, composed of six floors of office space follows a sinuous line which seems to embrace the white concrete dome that forms the external roof of the congress auditorium, the only eccentric exception in the entire complex.

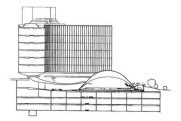

© Denis Esakov

architects	type	construction
Oscar Niemeyer, Paul Chemetov	istitutional	1971

45. Rue de Meaux Housing

Rue de Meaux
75021 Paris

external viewing only

2, 5, 7B > Jaurès
7B > Bolivar
5 > Laumière

48 > Rue de Meaux
26 > Marché Secrétan,
Jaurès - Stalingrad
**N13, N41, N45,
BUSM5** > Jaurès

At 64 Rue de Meaux, a short distance from Avenue Jean Jaurès in the 19th arrondissement in Paris, is the social housing residential complex designed by Pritzker Prize winning architect Renzo Piano and the RPBW team, and built between 1987 and 1991. This project is comprised of 220 social housing units and the architects were directly commissioned by the Régie immobilière de la Ville de Paris. It is composed of apartment buildings arranged around the perimeter of a large rectangular internal communal garden planted with shrubs and birch trees. With the exception of some of the smaller units, all of the apartments have a double aspect, one overlooking the gardens and another with views of the city. The building features a mixed facade composed of a double skin system. From the second to the seventh floor, the internal garden facades are comprised of 90×90 cm protruding grids made up of precast, fibreglass-reinforced concrete elements, inside which is an insulating layer, covered with terracotta tiles. The street facade surface is similar in shape and colour, but without the double skin system. Here, the cladding is attached directly to the primary structure. While the internal facades overlooking the garden still maintain their original appearance, the street facades were renovated between 2007 and 2009 to provide space for large glazed areas at ground level.

architects
Renzo Piano
Building Workshop

type
residential

construction
1991

46. Parc de la Villette

211 Avenue Jean Jaurès
75019 Paris

Tue - Sun / 10.30 am - 7.30 pm
+33 (0)1 40 03 75 75

lavillette.com

7 > Porte de la Villette
5 > Porte de Pantin

39, 71, 139, 150, 152
> Porte de la Villette
**75, 151, N13, N41,
N45, BUSM5** >
Porte de Pantin

T3b > Porte de Pantin -
Parc de La Villette

The result of a prestigious international competition, Bernard Tschumi's project for the Parc de la Villette, was incorporated within a much larger redevelopment plan, launched by the former president, François Mitterrand, aimed at revitalising an abandoned area in the north-east of Paris. Inaugurated in 1987, the project enabled the Swiss/French architect to demonstrate his de-constructivist architectural manifesto in a tangible form. Space, event and movement form the three basic elements, which, when rearranged with one another, embody the concept of Tschumi's project. Here they are interpreted through a structure that is broken up into different levels which interact with one another while maintaining compositional independence. The park is composed of three basic elements: lines, surfaces and points. The paths or lines cross the surfaces composed of paved or green areas on which the folies are built. These are small structures that act as reference points and form the architectural expression of the project. The red folies recall the aesthetics of Soviet constructivism but are different from one another in their architectural design. Most have no specific function other than confirming with their presence the concept of space as a place for potential spontaneous activities.

© Bernard Tschumi Architects

© Peter Mauss, courtesy of Bernard Tschumi Architects

architects
Bernard Tschumi

type
public space

construction
1987

47. Cité de la musique

221 Avenue Jean Jaurès
75019 Paris

Tue - Fri / 12 am - 6 pm
Sat - Sun / 10 am - 6 pm
+33 (0)1 44 84 44 84
contact@philharmoniedeparis.fr
philharmoniedeparis.fr

 5 > Porte de Pantin

 75, 151, N13, N41, N45, BUSM5 > Porte de Pantin

 T3b > Porte de Pantin - Parc de La Villette

The Cité de la musique is located at the southeast end of the Parc de La Villette. It was inaugurated on December 7, 1995, but since 2015 has been part of the larger Cité de la musique-Philarmonie de Paris complex. It was designed by Pritzker Prize winner, Christian de Portzamparc as a kind of "dreamlike town", grouping the Paris Conservatory, the Music Museum and several concert halls in a single building. It is a structure that invites the visitor to move with its flow, to explore the internal spaces that follow a labyrinth of circuits and walkways, multiplying the play of perspectives of the surrounding parkland. A fragmented composition of different structures fills the triangular site covering a total of almost 29,000 square metres. At the core of the building is a large concert hall able to seat between 900 and 1,600 spectators; the space can be adapted to different configurations according to the requirements of each performance. Other spaces include the underground amphitheatre for 250 spectators, and the Music Museum which houses a collection of musical instruments that date back to between the 16th and 21st centuries. The museum was designed by the French architect Franck Hammoutène. This "ideal City" of music also contains exhibition spaces, educational workshops, and a media library. To set the mood of this intriguing building, a red structure designed by Portzamparc marks the main entrance, a nod to the red *folies* by Tschumi.

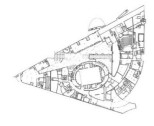

© Nicolas Borel

architects
Christian de Portzamparc

type
cultural

construction
1995

48. Philharmonie de Paris

221 Avenue Jean Jaurès
75019 Paris

Tue - Fri / 12 am - 6 pm
Sat - Sun / 10 am - 6 pm
+33 (0)1 44 84 44 85
contact@philharmoniedeparis.fr
philharmoniedeparis.fr

 5 > Porte de Pantin

 75, 151, N13, N41, N45, BUSM5 >
Porte de Pantin

 T3b > Porte de Pantin -
Parc de La Villette

To the visitor, the initial impact of the Philarmonie de Paris is the form of a mineral organism in motion, from its aluminium sheet cladding and bird shape mosaic in shades from grey to black, to the sinuous structure of the main concert hall in gleaming aluminium. The building by Ateliers Jean Nouvel was the winning project in the international competition to design a structure dedicated to music and culture, to complete the Cité de la Musique by Christian de Portzamparc set inside the Parc de la Villette by Bernard Tschumi, in the north-east of Paris. The heart of the building, the symphonic concert hall, was designed according to a new concept: flowing architecture without interruptions to envelope both musicians and public. Métra+Associés studio also collaborated in the conception and realization of the concert hall whose spatial continuity is proposed again on a greater scale in the relationship between the landscape and the architecture: visitors can take internal elevators, or follow a mountain path that zigzags up the north face of the building to enjoy unique views of the city.

© Ateliers Jean Nouvel – Métra+Associés

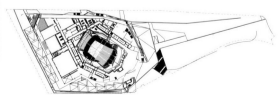

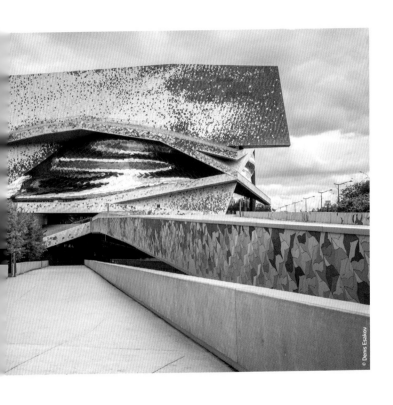

© Denis Esakov

architects
Ateliers Jean Nouvel,
Métra+Associés (concert hall)

type
cultural

construction
2015

49. *le*19M – Fashion Manufactury of Chanel

2 Place Skanderbeg
75019 Paris

Wed - Fri / 11 am - 6 pm
Sat - Sun / 11 am - 7 pm

info@le19m.fr
www.le19m.com

 RER E > Rosa Parks

 35, 45, 239 >
Parc du Millénaire

 T3b > Porte
d'Aubervilliers

In the north of Paris, on the edge of the working class suburb of Aubervilliers, the Chanel fashion house decided to build a new single headquarter to house its Métiers d'Art: the handcrafting workshops that work with Chanel, all the major names of luxury, and young fashion designers. The architects also created exhibition and events spaces for contact with the public. *le*19M building takes its name from the 19th arrondissement where it is located, while M represents the many aspects linked with high fashion in French: Mode, Maison and Métiers. Rudy Ricciotti created the structure (five floors plus two levels below ground) with a strikingly individual facade composed of slim vertical elements arranged in varying configurations, interwoven to represent the complex structure of textile warp and weave.

architects
Rudy Ricciotti

type
multi-purpose

construction
2021

50. Les Orgues de Flandre

69-95 Avenue de Flandre
75019 Paris

external viewing only

 7 > Riquet, Crimée

 54, N42 > Crimée
**45, Traverse Ney
Flandre** > Curial -
Archereau

This complex was designed between 1973 and 1980 by the German architect, Martin van Treeck, who was also a student of the French architect, Jean Ginsberg. The social housing complex is composed of different buildings, mostly set along Avenue de Flandre: the main buildings are 15 storeys high, and are dominated by four towers called Prélude, Fuge, Sonate, and Cantate. The buildings create a boundary between the avenue and a large 2.5 acre public park that is surrounded by residential buildings. The four towers are 82, 96, 104 and 123 metres high respectively, and stand out in the midst of the neighbouring urban fabric while the main buildings were designed in almost sculptural form by the architect: they were the subject of formal and structural experimentation; composed of levels that are progressively projected or recessed on the facade, they confer a multi-faceted effect that lightens the imposing mass of the overall design.

Lorenzo Zandri © 2017

architects
Martin van Treeck

type
residential

construction
1980

51. Student Residence

65 Rue Philippe de Girard
75018 Paris

external viewing only

www.crous-paris.fr/logement/
residence-pajol-2

2 > La Chapelle
12 > Marx Dormoy

Traverse Ney Flandre >
Pajol - Departement,
La Chapelle
35, 45, 48 > Place
de La Chapelle

This student residence, designed by the French-Italian firm LAN Architecture, is located on the corner of Rue Philippe de Girard and Rue Pajol in an urban area of the La Chapelle district in the 18th arrondissement in Paris. The project design is composed of an organic layout of constructed volumes and open voids, and is skilfully integrated within the diversified fabric of the surrounding quarter. The architecture is based on the juxtaposition of several residential blocks designed to house 143 furnished student rooms of different types. In contrast with the solid street facade, the residential blocks enclose an internal courtyard, the heart of the project, 225 square metres, which defines the correlation between the buildings and provides a space for students to relax and socialise. It could be said that the project is designed with a dual objective: on one hand, externally, it establishes the integration within the surrounding urban fabric while creating an inward-looking space, on the other. This is highlighted by the careful choice of materials employed for the facades: the street frontages are faced with austere dark, slate-coloured brick, while the internal walls are clad with light larch-wood slats.

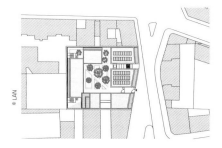
© LAN

architects
LAN

type
residential

construction
2011

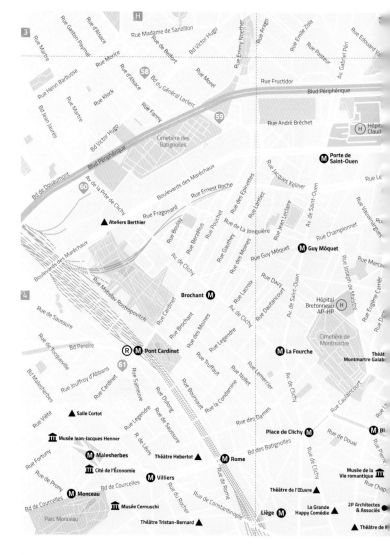

0 m   200 m   500 m

Châteauform'
Les Docks de Paris ▲

Cimetière parisien
de La Chapelle

Blvd Périphérique

Rue des Rosiers

Av. Michelet

Rue Paul Bert

Rue René Binet

Rue Jean Cocteau

Rue des Poissonniers

Porte de la Chapelle Arena ♟

Boulevards des Maréchaux

Ⓜ Porte de
la Chapelle

Rue de la Chapelle

Rue Boucry

Ⓜ Porte de
Clignancourt

Rue Belliard

Boulevards des Maréchaux

Rue Belliard

Rue du Poteau

♟ Hôtel Kyriad
Porte de Clignancourt

Rue Champorget

Rue Championnet

Rue Champ...

Rue Duhesme

Théâtre Pixel ▲

Bd Ornano

Rue Letort

Rue du Ruisseau

▲ Théâtre des
Béliers Parisiens

Ⓜ Simplon

54

Rue du Simplon

Bd Ornano

Rue Montcalm

Rue du Poteau

Rue des Cloys

Rue Ordener

Rue Hermel

Rue Binod

Trottin Architectes

Rue Marcadet

Rue Simart

Ⓜ Marcadet
Poissonniers

▲ Le Funambule

Rue Ramey

Rue Marcadet

ck Ⓜ Lamarck-Caulaincourt

ulaincourt

Rue Lamarck

Rue Custine

Bd Barbès

Rue d'Oran

Rue Saint-Vincent

Rue Doudeauville

Rue Léon

D

🏛 Musée de Montmartre

Ⓜ Château Rouge

Place du Tertre 📷

✚ Basilique du
Sacré-Cœur de Montmartre

Bd Barbès

📷 Place
Émile Goudeau

📷 Vue de Paris

Rue de Clignancourt

Rue Polonceau

Audran

FGO-Barbara ▲

Ⓜ Abbesses

Ⓜ Barbès-Rochechouart

Le Trianon ▲

Ⓜ Anvers

Hôpital
Lariboisière Ⓗ
AP-HP

Ⓜ Pigalle

R. des Martyrs

Rue du Delta

Victor Massé

Aveue Trudaine

Rue Petrelle

● Chatillon Architectes

Rue Condorcet

Rue Turgot

Gare du Nord ⓂⓇ

Rue de Navarin

Rue de Maubeuge

Ⓜ Saint-Georges

● RSHP France

Montmartre,
Clichy, Saint-Denis
[9, 18 arr.]

52. Pigalle Duperré
53. Tristan Tzara House
54. La Piscine des Amiraux
55. National Archives of France
56. Saint-Denis Pleyel
Railway Station
57. The Olympic and
Paralympic Village –
Paris 2024 Île-Saint-Denis
58. Maison du Peuple de Clichy
59. Tour Bois-le-Prêtre
60. Paris Courthouse
61. 40 Housing Units

52. Pigalle Duperré

22 Rue Duperré
75009 Paris

Mon - Fri / 12 am - 7 pm
Sat / 10 am - 6 pm
Sun / 11 am - 5 pm

 2, 12 > Pigalle

 30, 40, 54, N01, N02 > Pigalle
30, 54, 74, N01 > Blanche

The original basketball court project created in collaboration between Ill-Studio and Pigalle and Nike brands, is set inside an irregular empty urban space in the 9th arrondissement in Paris. This operation was inspired partly as a marketing initiative, but the concept has enormous potential for utilizing empty urban spaces between buildings which, with limited intervention, can be transformed into new symbolic areas representative of local neighbourhood communities. The interesting aspect of this small intervention for transforming a public space, also relies on the fact that the lines and colours which are the main focal point, can be updated and modified very rapidly. Since the first project was designed in 2009, the space has been transformed five times in various versions, with the most recent in blended fluo colours and geometrical designs to provide a range of captivating graphical solutions with great visual impact.

architects
III-Studio

type
public space

construction
2017

53. Tristan Tzara House

15 Avenue Junot
75018 Paris

external viewing only

 12 > Lamarck - Caulaincourt

 40 > 88 Rue Lepic, Moulin de La Galette
80 > Lamarck - Caulaincourt

This house was designed by the Austrian architect, Adolf Loos, the pioneer of the Modernist movement. It is located in Montmartre, at 15 Avenue Junot in the 18th arrondissement, and was built between 1925 and 1927 for the Romanian poet, Tristan Tzara, and his wife, the artist, Greta Knutson. The project is based on a plain and simple design, clear and symmetrical, entirely devoid of any form of decoration, in agreement with the principles laid out by Loos in his most famous book, *Ornament and Crime*. The strict main facade is perfectly geometrical, divided horizontally by the surface materials: the lower floors are clad in stone, while the upper section has a light-coloured plaster finish. The ground floor was designed as a rental apartment, while the upper floors contained the actual residence of the clients.

architects
Adolf Loos

type
residential

construction
1927

54. La Piscine des Amiraux

6 Rue Hermann-Lachapelle
75018 Paris

Mon / 7 am - 8.30 am,
4.30 pm - 10.30 pm
Tue, Thu / 7 am - 8.30 am,
11.30 am - 1.30 pm
Wed / 7 am - 8.30 am,
11.30 am - 7.00 pm
Fri / 11.30 am - 1.30 pm
Sat / 7 am - 6 pm
Sun / 8 am - 6 pm
+33 (0)1 46 06 46 47

www.paris.fr/lieux/piscine-des-
amiraux-2944

 4 > Simplon
4, 12 > Marcadet -
Poissonniers

 85 > Albert Kahn
56, N14, N44 >
Simplon
302 > Marcadet -
Poissonniers

Enclosed within a residential complex flanked by Rue Hermann Lachapelle to the south, and Rue des Amiraux to the north in the 18th arrondissement in Paris, the Amiraux swimming pool is one of the oldest in the city. The complex dates back to the 1920s and is one of the most fascinating projects designed by the architect Henri Sauvage, commissioned by the Paris municipal department for affordable housing. The building was designed in 1913, but the overall project was completed only after the First World War between 1922 and 1927, while the swimming pool was finished in 1930. The residential complex features tiered terraced facades that allow each of the 80 housing units a maximum of natural daylight. The swimming pool is located in the core of the building and is lit by natural light thanks to the glass roofing which also covers the internal courtyard of the apartment building. The entire project was designed in late Art Deco style, but with the infiltration of additional features influenced by the more recent Bauhaus style.

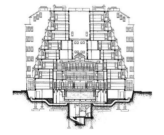

© Antoine Mercusot

architects
Henri Sauvage /
Chatillon Architectes
(restoration)

type
sport

construction
1927 / 2017

55. National Archives of France

59 Rue Guynemer
93383 Pierrefitte-sur-Seine
cedex

Mon - Sat / 9 am - 4.45 pm
+33 (0) 1 75 47 20 00
contact.archives-
nationales@culture.gouv.fr
www.archives-nationales.
culture.gouv.fr

13 > St-Denis
Université

**168, 256, 268, 353,
356** > Saint-Denis -
Université
168, 253, 256, 268 >
Toussaint Louverture

T5 > Guynemer

The National Archives were created during the French Revolution, and contain documents dating back from the 7th century to the present day. They include milestones of French history such as the Merovingian papyrus, the trials of the Knights Templar, the diary of Louis XVI, the will and testament of Napoleon, and the Declaration of the Rights of Man and the Citizen. The imposing monolithic main structure houses the archival documents and reading room. This "stronghold" is completely clad with an aluminium skin that covers the entire facade except for a few glazed inserts that increase the natural light in the reading room and the entrance route. Alongside the sculptural building is a large basin that acts as a reflecting pool. Several suspended walkways connect the main block with other smaller cantilevered buildings, projecting sharply in perpendicular directions towards the city and supported on slender pillars. These structures house office spaces, the conference room, and an exhibition hall. The facades are mainly glazed to give a permeable impression in open contrast with the explicit enclosure of the archive space. A diamond shaped pattern is featured throughout the complex, repeated in the continuous aluminium cladding and along the "satellite" buildings. A landscaped green route by Florence Mercier introduces and guides the visitor into the complex with alternating shapes, forms, colours and shades, to complete the architectural effect.

© Archivio Fuksas, Courtesy Studio Fuksas

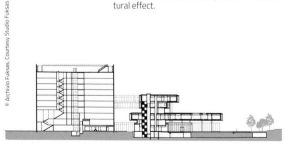

© Roland Halbe, Courtesy Studio Fuksas

architects
Studio Fuksas

type
administrative

construction
2013

56. Saint-Denis Pleyel Railway Station

39 Boulevard Ornano
93200 Saint-Denis

open to the public

14 > Saint-Denis-Pleyel
13 > Carrefour Pleyel

RER D > Stade de
France - Saint Denis

139, 255 >
Docteur Finot
139, 274, N44 >
Carrefour Pleyel
139, 173 >
Landy - Pleyel

The Saint-Denis Pleyel railway station is part of the far greater urban infrastructure, Grand Paris Express, which will be completed in 2030 with over 200 kilometres of metropolitan train lines and 68 new stations. One of the new stations was designed by the team of the Japanese architect, Kengo Kuma. Built on a 9,000 square metre site, it will be the main transport hub for the north of Paris, the converging point for Lines 14, 15 and 16/17 of the Grand Paris Express. The structure has been designed as a vast urban space spread over 9 floors, four of which are underground. Continuous access to all areas of the space permits the public to use the interiors, with all the services required of a large railway station, as well as the external spaces thanks to pedestrian routes across the roof: a series of ramps connect the different levels to create overhead walkways. Light plays an essential part in this project thanks to the vast glazed surfaces and the central atrium that acts as junction for all passenger routes. The complex also includes a cultural programme and a retail space. A 250 metre pedestrian and cycling bridge will enable the public to cross the railway tracks to access the RER D. Kuma's design is aimed at overcoming the urban fragmentation of the area, by providing a public plaza, roofed multi-level public space, and an urban network in a single coherent context.

© Kengo Kuma & Associates

© Kengo Kuma & Associates by L'autre Image

architects
Kengo Kuma & Associates

type
infrastructural

construction
2024

57. The Olympic and Paralympic Village –
Paris 2024 Île-Saint-Denis

33 Quai du Châtelier
93450 Île-Saint-Denis

open to the public

www.paris2024.org/en/the-
olympic-and-paralympic-village

 13 > Carrefour Pleyel

 139 > Rue Ampère
139, 274, N44 >
Carrefour Pleyel

The creation of the Olympic village has transformed an area lacking in identity into a territory full of new possibilities; the project represents just the first stage in establishing a new central focus in the metropolitan area. This portion of the city spans the three districts of the Île-Saint-Denis, Saint-Denis and Saint-Ouen-sur-Seine previously occupied by industrial parks but rich in natural resources. One of the requirements that inspired Dominique Perrault's masterplan was to take advantage of the Seine as an element to connect and reinforce the "mixed" nature of the area, proposing an athletes' village, not built as a brand new project, but designed to reduce environmental impact, by using pre-existing structures like the old electrical power plant, converted to house the Cité du Cinema. More than 14,250 Olympic athletes and 8,000 para-athletes will be housed in over 80 buildings surrounded by planted green areas, ramps and access points to the river. After the games, beginning in November 2024, the village will become an authentic neighbourhood-style district, with family and student accommodation, a hotel, commercial activities, stores and office spaces, for a total surface area of 52,000 square metres. The overall project is aimed at creating long-term development and a reduction in the social difference between the centre of Paris and the outlying suburbs.

© Dominique Perrault architecte_Adagp

Source : Dominique Perrault Architecte_Adagp

architects
Dominique Perrault

type
multi-purpose

construction
2024

58. Maison du Peuple de Clichy

7 Rue Martissot
92110 Clichy

external viewing only

 14 > Saint-Ouen

 RER C > Saint-Ouen

 66, 74, 173 > Général Leclerc - Victor Hugo
Tuc > Maison du Peuple

La Maison du Peuple was designed by the architects Marcel Lods and Eugène Beaudouin, with the collaboration of the engineer Vladimir Bodiansky and Jean Prouvé. It was built in Clichy (Hauts-de-Seine) between 1935 and 1939, and is located just outside the Boulevard Périphérique ring road, north west of Paris. The building was designed as a multi-functional structure for public use, including a covered market, trade union meeting rooms, office spaces, a conference hall, and a cinema. The building was constructed entirely in steel and glass, with a plain rectangular design as the designers focussed their attention on the internal spaces and their capacity to accommodate the different requirements of the building. In answer to the need for flexibility in the internal spaces, the team experimented with mechanized methods using sliding partitions, removable flooring, and a retractable roof. Many extremely innovative technical and technological solutions were adopted, not only internally, but also for the exterior of the building. For the first time, Prouvé used a system of non-load-bearing curtain walls. Today the structure is undergoing renovation supervised by Jouin Manku and Perrot & Richard Architects. The building will retain its multi-function aspect, mainly housing gastronomical activities. As well as the covered market, it will house the Alain Ducasse culinary workshops, including an exhibition space, a restaurant, "Bouillon", and a "chef's table". Although the internal spaces will be widely renovated, the structure will undergo faithful conservative restoration to maintain its original appearance. Elements of the pre-existing structure will be salvaged, classified according to the level of disrepair, and restored where possible, accentuating the unique original lighting engineering.

© Images Artefactorylab pour Jouin Manku et Perrot&Richard

architects
Marcel Lods, Eugène
Beaudouin, Jean Prouvé,
Vladimir Bodiansky /
Jouin Manku, Perrot & Richard
Architects (restoration)

type
multi-purpose

construction
1939 / ongoing

59. Tour Bois-le-Prêtre

5 Boulevard du Bois le Prêtre
75017 Paris

external viewing only

 13, 14 > Porte de Clichy

 RER C > Porte de Clichy

 66, 341 > Bois Le Prêtre

 T3b > Epinettes - Pouchet

Built between 1959 and 1962, and designed by the architect, Raymond Lopez, this social housing tower block in the northern suburbs of Paris, is an imposing vertical structure, over 50 metres high, containing around a hundred apartments. The initial project, built in the sixties using an innovative prefabricated construction system, was almost destined for demolition due to severe deterioration. In the early 2000s, it was considered for a design competition launched by the city council, aimed at restoring and upgrading the building. In 2005, the competition was won by a team composed of the Lacaton & Vassal architectural firm, and Frédéric Druot. Their project resulted in a low-key but harmonious solution that strongly changed the urban perception of the Lopez building. More specifically, the architects focussed on extending the existing apartment floor plans with the addition of self-supporting balconies and closable terrace-conservatories which increased the surfaces of the living rooms and communal spaces. This solution has given a far more contemporary appearance to the facades, dominated by large glazed surfaces, in contrast with the pre-existing windows.

© Lacaton & Vassal

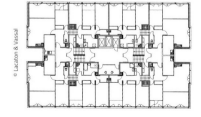

architects
Raymond Lopez /
Frédéric Druot,
Lacaton & Vassal

type
residential

construction
1962 / 2011

60. Paris Courthouse

Parvis du tribunal de Paris
75017 Paris

Mon - Fri / 8.30 am - 6 pm
+33 (0)1 44 32 51 51

www.cours-appel.justice.fr/paris

 13, 14 > Porte
de Clichy

 RER C > Porte de Clichy

 54, 74 > Boulay
28, 54, 138, 173 >
Porte de Clichy

 T3b > Porte de Clichy -
Tribunal de Paris

On the northern edge of Paris, opposite the Martin Luther King Park, stands the new Paris Courthouse complex designed by the Renzo Piano Building Workshop team. The large 6,000 square metre plaza which overlooks Avenue de la Porte-de-Clichy provides access to the podium base that houses the largest law court complex in Europe. This contains the entrance atriums (one central and two lateral) all of which give almost entirely unrestricted views thanks to the glass facades. This is not simply a design choice; while the architecture allows the public to view activities in progress within the building, it also symbolises the transparency of Justice. All the open walkways on the upper floors overlook the full-height ground floor atriums. The podium base structure of the complex houses 90 court rooms, while the upper floors which form the 160 metre tower, contain office spaces and meeting rooms for magistrates, public prosecutors, and judges. The stacked, decreasingly-sized, blocks are separated from each other by horizontal cantilevered divisions. Externally, the tiered separations are visible thanks to the horizontal elements that provide shade and landscaped green terraces. A vertical "spinal column" connects all the buildings and contains the stairs and elevators, while providing panoramic views of the city. As with all Renzo Piano projects, the technology used in this "vertical city" is focussed on maximum energy saving techniques, necessary for the efficient operation of such a vast judicial complex.

© Renzo Piano Building Workshop

architects
Renzo Piano
Building Workshop

type
institutional

construction
2017

61. 40 Housing Units

3 Rue Georges Picquart
75017 Paris

external viewing only

 14 > Pont Cardinet

 L, Transilien L >
Pont Cardinet
T3b > Marguerite Long

 28, 94 > Pont Cardinet

With its design for the 40 residential apartments in the Clichy-Batignolles urban development plan, LAN has openly addressed the subject of Parisian residential housing as a homage to Haussmann architecture. The aim is to interpret the fundamental Haussmann core elements of flexibility and perpetuation in a contemporary style, maintaining the same capacity for durability over time. The footprint of the building was dictated by the triangular form of the corner plot, the meeting point between two streets and two different urban fabrics. Precise geometrical scansion is a major external feature where the windows and loggias of identical size and alignment are repeated across the entire facade with strict geometrical regularity. The structural clarity visible in Haussmann architecture can be seen in all facades: all four maintain the same regular alignment with only a few variations according to sun exposure. While the constant repetition of the identical window pattern and facade surface hints at spatial flexibility on one hand, it does not give any idea of the specific use of individual internal spaces, reinforced even further by the formal appearance of the building.

© LAN

architects
LAN

type
residential

construction
2014

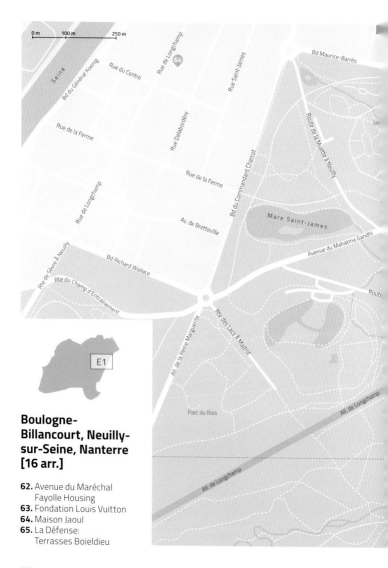

Boulogne-Billancourt, Neuilly-sur-Seine, Nanterre [16 arr.]

62. Avenue du Maréchal Fayolle Housing
63. Fondation Louis Vuitton
64. Maison Jaoul
65. La Défense: Terrasses Boieldieu

Rue Jacques Dulud

Rue Charles Laffitte

Rue Jacques Dulud

Av. Charles de Gaulle

Bd Maurice-Barrès

Rue Charles Laffitte

Bd des Sablons

Bd Maurice-Barrès

Bd Maurice-Barrès

Fondation
Louis Vuitton

Avenue du Mahatma Gandhi

Rte de Prte des Sablons à la Prte Maillot

Pavillon d'Armenoville 📷

All. de Longchamp

Blvd Périphérique

Rte de la Prte Dauphine à la Prte des Sablons

All. de Longchamp

Blvd Périphérique

Bd de l'Amiral Bruix

Pavillon Dauphine 📷
SAINTCLAIR

Porte Dauphine Ⓜ

Av. Foch

All. des Poteaux

Ⓡ Avenue Foch

Musée de la Contrefaçon 🏛

All. Saint-Denis

Rte de Suresnes

Neuilly

📷 Pavillon Royal

Blvd Périphérique

Bd Lannes

62

Rue du Général Appert

Rue Dufrenoy

Rue Spontini

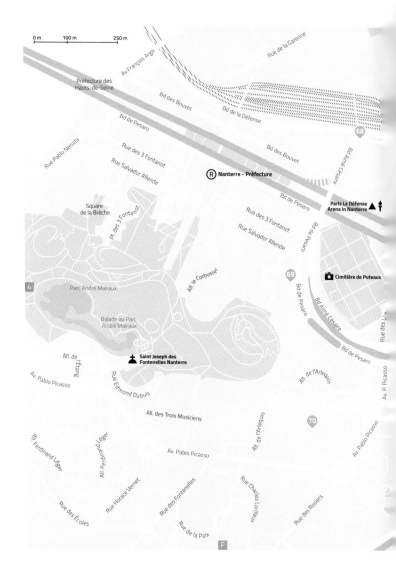

0 m   100 m   250 m

Préfecture des
Hauts-de-Seine

Av François Argo

Rue de la Garenne

Bd des Bouvet

Bd de la Défense

Bd de Pesaro

Bd des Bouvet

Rue Pablo Neruda

Rue des 3 Fontanot

Rue Salvador Allende

68

® Nanterre - Préfecture

Bd de Pesaro

Bd Aimé Césaire

Square
de la Brèche

Pl. des 3 Fontanot

Rue des 3 Fontanot

Rue Salvador Allende

Paris La Défense
Arena in Nanterre

Bd de Pesaro

4

Parc André Malraux

All. le Corbusier

69

Cimitière de Puteaux

Bd Aimé Césaire

Balade au Parc
André Malraux

Bd de Pesaro

Rue des Lo

All. de l'Étang

Saint Joseph des
Fontenelles Nanterre

Av. Pablo Picasso

Rue Edmond Dubuis

All. de l'Arlequin

Av. P. Picasso

All. des Trois Musiciens

70

All. Ferdinand Léger

All. Ferdinand Léger

Av. Pablo Picasso

All. de l'Arlequin

Av. Pablo Picasso

Rue Horace Vernet

Rue des Écoles

Rue des Fontenelles

Rue Charles Lorilleux

Rue des Rosiers

Rue de la Paix

F

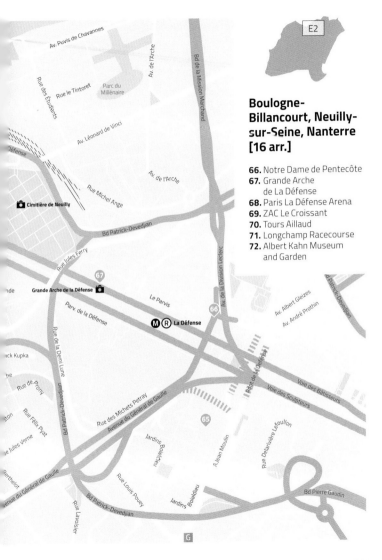

E2

Boulogne-Billancourt, Neuilly-sur-Seine, Nanterre [16 arr.]

66. Notre Dame de Pentecôte
67. Grande Arche de La Défense
68. Paris La Défense Arena
69. ZAC Le Croissant
70. Tours Aillaud
71. Longchamp Racecourse
72. Albert Kahn Museum and Garden

Av. Puvis de Chavannes

Av. de l'Arche

Bd de la Mission Marchand

Rue des Étudiants

Rue le Tintoret

Parc du Millénaire

Défense

Av. Léonard de Vinci

Av. de l'Arche

Rue Michel Ange

Cimitière de Neuilly

Bd Patrick-Devedjian

Rue Jules Ferry

Grande Arche de la Défense

Le Parvis

Av. de la Division Leclerc

nde

Parv. de la Défense

Rue de la Demi Lune

ack Kupka

Rue de Prony

Bd Patrick-Devedjian

Rue Félix Pyat

Rue Jules Verne

herthelot

Avenue du Général de Gaulle

Rue Lavoisier

Bd Patrick-Devedjian

Rue des Michets Petray

Avenue du Général de Gaulle

Jardins Boieldieu

Rue Louis Pouey

Jardins Boieldieu

A. Jean Moulin

Rue Delarivière Lefoullon

Bd Pierre Gaudin

Av. Albert Gleizes

Av. André Prothin

Rdpt de La Défense

Voie des Sculpteurs

Voie des Batisseurs

ton

M R La Défense

G

62. Avenue du Maréchal Fayolle Housing

Avenue du Maréchal Fayolle
75016 Paris

external viewing only

 RER C > Avenue Henri Martin

 PC > Dufrenoy

 T3b > Porte Dauphine (Avenue Foch)

This social housing project was created in the 16th arrondissement district near the Bois de Boulogne by the Japanese award-winning architects SANAA. Four separate buildings form the basic structural design creating interesting spatial relationships. Internal and external connecting spaces provide access and integrate the residential buildings with the flow of the surrounding urban space. The curving facades create organic forms, while providing apartments with multiple urban views and perspectives, as well as a dynamic layout for general circulation. The ground floor pilotis support structure provides access from street level; the encased spaces are recessed compared to the upper facades, and the semi-transparent metal mesh enclosures contain bicycle storage, entrances and reception areas. On the upper floors, the variations in shape and form provide the possibility of different internal layouts and design for the 100 residential apartments.

© SANAA

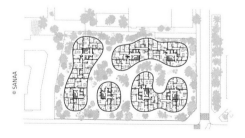

architects
SANAA

type
residential

construction
2018

63. Fondation Louis Vuitton

8 Avenue du Mahatma Gandhi
75016 Paris

Mon, Wed - Fri / 12 pm - 7 pm
Sat - Sun / 11 am - 8 pm
+33 (0)1 40 69 96 00
fondationlouisvuitton@
brunswickgroup.com
www.fondationlouisvuitton.fr

 1 > Les Sablons

 63, 244 > Fondation
L.Vuitton

Located in the heart of the Bois de Boulogne, the Fondation Louis Vuitton was inaugurated in October, 2014 after years of 3D project research and development. The striking building, commissioned by the LVMH group and designed by Canadian starchitect Frank Gehry, represents a new Parisian landmark and was created as a vast cultural centre that includes eleven exhibition spaces and a large auditorium that can seat between 360 and 1,000 spectators. The art centre emerges boldly from the dense vegetation of the surrounding wooded park, with its eye-catching glass roofing composed of overlapping curved structures that evoke yacht sails. The vast glass sails envelop the functional heart of the building concealing the distribution of the internal spaces whose complex arrangement can be fully discerned only in cross-section.

© Frank Gehry

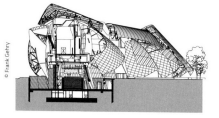

© Iwan Baan

architects
Frank Gehry

type
cultural

construction
2014

64. Maison Jaoul

81 Rue de Longchamp
92200 Neuilly-sur-Seine

external viewing only
+33 (0)1 42 88 75 72
reservation@
fondationlecorbusier.fr
www.fondationlecorbusier.fr

 43, 93 > Rue du Centre

This project for a double residence in the neighbourhood of Neuilly-sur-Seine, just outside the Boulevard Périphérique in the north-west of Paris, was built by Le Corbusier between 1951 and 1956. The two adjacent houses are built on a single plot overlooking Rue de Longchamp, and are arranged at right angles to one another, the first parallel to the street, and the other at the rear of the garden. The twin houses have the same architectural style, in both their main features and external finishes. The facade materials (raw concrete, exposed brick, and wooden detailing) were left bare to underline their simplicity. The striking aspect of this later residential project by Le Corbusier is the total abandon of the fundamental Modernist principles that were typical of his earlier projects. Like some of his other later designs, this project is testament to a more Brutalist and expressive approach, that was to culminate in the formal experimentation for his Chandigarh project, built at the same time, or for his renowned Sainte Marie de La Tourette design.

architects
Le Corbusier

type
residential

construction
1955

65. La Défense: Terrasses Boieldieu

100 Terrasse Boieldieu
92800 Puteaux

open to the public

 1 > La Défense

 RER A > La Défense

 73, 174, N24 >
Boieldieu

The Terrasses Boieldieu public space project, designed by a team led by Empreinte, was inaugurated in Puteaux, in the Défense district in 2018. In a neighbourhood that was developed beginning in the 1960s, and composed of a combination of office blocks and retail space, there was a strong need for a restoration strategy to improve the public spaces and to provide a general upgrade for the urban surroundings. The project was aimed at reconnecting with nature with a new design for green landscaped spaces; the 16,000 square metre area has been planted with about 80 new trees, and more than 3,500 square metres of green landscaping. Concrete slab paving (50×120 cm) has been laid to unify the plaza and to resolve the serious water infiltration problems present in the existing terraces where slabs had deteriorated in the green areas. A suspended steel walkway has resolved the difference in height between street level and the public space area, making it accessible to the public. Two separate green areas divide the terraces: le Jardin des Continents and le Jardin Suspendu. The first is open to the public and provides a relaxing space with seating benches and shady areas. The Jardin Suspendu is an area reserved for the local residents who wish to take part in gardening workshops.

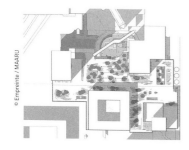

© Empreinte / MAARU

© Empreinte

architects
Empreinte, Pierre Gangnet,
MAARU, Igrec Ingénierie,
L.E.A.

type
public space

construction
2019

66. Notre Dame de Pentecôte

1 Avenue de la Division Leclerc
92800 Puteaux

Mon - Tue, Thu - Fri /
8 am - 2.30 pm
Wed / 8 am - 7 pm
+33 (0)1 47 75 83 25
ecrire@ndp92.fr
ndp92.fr

 1 > La Défense

 RER A, RER L, RER U >
La Défense

 73, 178, N24 >
La Défense

 T2 > La Défense
(Grande Arche)

Notre Dame de Pentecôte was opened in 2001, in the heart of the financial district of the Défense, in the Hauts-de-Seine Department. This project, designed by the architect Franck Hammoutène, represents an original example of the reinterpretation of a religious space, in contemporary style. A large translucent glass wall perpendicular to the facade, bears the silhouette of a Christian cross, identifying the building at the entrance, and forms the first of a series of thresholds leading to the internal space. The structure and layout of the building are geometrically simple and minimalist; the complexity lies in the internal arrangement spread over the three floors of the main building. The principle activities are organised in a vertical system: the upper liturgical chamber, the reception entrance and social space, and the meeting rooms. As well as providing a space dedicated to prayer, this building was designed as a meeting place for the local community; in fact, other activities include exhibitions, workshops, meetings and training courses.

© Giulia Ceretani

architects
Franck Hammoutène

type
religious

construction
2001

67. Grande Arche de La Défense

1 Parvis de la Défense
92800 Puteaux

Mon - Sun / 10 am - 7 pm

 1 > La Défense

 **RER A, RER L, RER U** >
La Défense

 73, 178, N24 >
La Défense
163, 276 >
Les Terrasses
160, 163, 259, N53 >
Esplanade Charles
de Gaulle

 T2 > La Défense
(Grande Arche)

The Grande Arche de La Défense is located on the prolongation of the Historic Axis that began with the construction of the Champs-Élysées and was designed as an extension of the monumental axis of Paris into the north-west sector of the city. The Danish architect, Otto von Spreckelsen was inspired by the monumental tradition of the triumphal arch for the building erected in the business district of La Défense. Inaugurated in 1989 for the bi-centenary of the French Revolution, its design effaces and stylises the traditional decorative model of triumphal arches, but maintains the monumental scale and the refined quality of the construction materials. The huge portal forms a hypercube, hollowed in the centre to create a splayed frame, 110 metres high, 108 metres wide, and 112 metres deep, faced with pale marble.

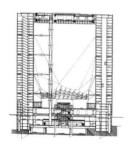

© Denis Esakov

architects
Johann Otto von Spreckelsen

type
multi-purpose

construction
1989

68. Paris La Défense Arena

8 Rue des Sorins
92000 Nanterre

open only during public events

www.parisladefense-arena.com

 1 > La Défense

 RER A, RER L, RER U >
La Défense
RER A > Nanterre-
Préfecture

 163, 276 >
Les Terrasses
160, 163, 259, N53 >
Esplanade Charles
de Gaulle

 T2 > La Défense
(Grande Arche)

The Défense Arena was opened in 2017, and sits at the foot of the Grande Arche de La Défense in Nanterre, a metropolitan suburb north-west of Paris. The arena was designed as part of the far larger territorial development project called "Seine-Arche". The arena was designed as a multi-purpose arena to host indoor sports events and concerts. Conceived as a modular space, it covers a total space of 94,000 square metres, and the main area is famous for its unprecedented capacity, with seating for 40,000 for concerts, and 30,000 for sports matches. The building also includes 31,000 square metres of office space occupied by the Hauts-de-Seine administration, retail stores and restaurants. The control of the large scale structure and its integration within the surrounding urban fabric was one of the major aspects in its construction, cleverly resolved by the French architect Christian de Portzamparc, who adopted a gently curving shape, focussing on horizontal rather than vertical lines. This aspect, as well as the giant semi-transparent aluminium and glass scales of the facade help to reduce the visual impact of the vast structure.

© Christian de Portzamparc | 2Portzamparc

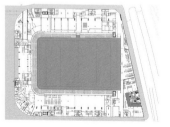

© Nicolas Borel

architects
Christian de Portzamparc

type
sport

construction
2017

69. ZAC Le Croissant

50 Boulevard de Pesaro
92000 Nanterre

open to the public

 1 > La Défense

 RER A, RER L, RER U >
La Défense
RER A > Nanterre-
Préfecture

 163, 276 >
Les Terrasses
160, 163, 259, N53 >
Esplanade Charles
de Gaulle

With a design concept that reflects the dynamic and diverse identity of the neighbourhood, this urban park, set in a space between buildings from the seventies and eighties and new urban settlements, offers versatile and original attractions and assumes a new social and spatial significance. The former vehicle scale is now replaced by that of the pedestrian: the ground level, once only accessible as residents' parking is now full of activity. To encourage and enhance diversity, accessibility, and functionality, the project hosts a collection of diverse elements that propose innovative ways to use the public space, all with unique common characteristics: they are original, they come from different contexts and have multiple functions. Curved ping-pong tables from Singapore and eye-catching litter bins from the Netherlands sit alongside more familiar objects like exercise equipment, table football, park stools and benches. The white markings on the black asphalt suggest games with flexible rules, inviting users to use the guides however they wish. The trees were selected from all over the world and carefully placed to ensure their adjustment to local conditions. A system of "green basins" is positioned all over the site to collect surface water run-off and filter it through the vegetation before it percolates into the water table below.

© Topotek 1

© Hans Joosten

architects
Topotek 1

type
public space

construction
2020

70. Tours Aillaud

Allée de l'Arlequin
92000 Nanterre

Mon - Wed, Fri / 9 am - 12 pm,
1 pm - 5.30 pm
Thu / 1 pm - 5.30 pm
Sat / 9 am - 12.30 pm

 1 > La Défense -
Grande Arche

 159, 163 > Les Rosiers

The Tours Aillaud are a group of towers that form the residential complex in the Pablo Picasso quarter in Nanterre, on the north-west boundary of Paris. This project, also called Tours Nuages, was undoubtedly one of the most original complexes built in the "Glorious thirty years" between 1945 and 1975, when, during an economic expansion, the French government invested heavily in public social housing schemes. The complex, composed of eighteen tower blocks, was built between 1974 and 1981, and was designed by the architect Émile Aillaud, with the collaboration of the engineer, Ashton Azaïs, and the artist, Fabio Rieti. The name Tours Nuages, (literally "Cloud towers") partially refers to the formal connotation, and to the dreamlike and playful atmosphere of the project. The buildings have gently curving lines, and facades decorated with glass paste mosaics. The facades also feature large-scale windows in three different configurations: circles, tear-drop shapes, and squares with rounded corners.

architects
Émile Aillaud

type
residential

construction
1976

71. Longchamp Racecourse

61 Route des Tribunes
75016 Paris

open to the public
+33 (0)1 49 10 20 65
commercial@
parislongchamp.com
www.parislongchamp.com

241, 43 > Hippodrome
de Longchamp
244, 70 > Les Moulins
- Camping

The Longchamp Racecourse is one of the most prestigious in France and among the most famous in the world. Immortalized by Manet and Degas, the 19th century structure is set in the Bois de Boulogne, and is host to the famous Prix de L'Arc de Triomphe race that attracts up to 60,000 spectators a year. The Dominique Perrault architectural firm was commissioned with the renovation of the race course, and designed the overall complex like a landscape to provide a setting to enhance the historical buildings and offer new views over the city. Work has begun to demolish, remodel and create new functions for certain buildings alongside the new constructions. The new design features a streamlined gold-coloured structure of overlapping sloping terraces that provide excellent views of the race track. The top-level grandstand "slides" outwards, creating an overhanging projection over the rest of the building in a leap towards the finish line. All guest areas are connected by a pedestrian walkway, called "les Planches", equipped with metal elements for shade along the whole promenade, to recall the tree-lined streets of Paris.

© Dominique Perrault architecte_Adagp

© Vincent Fillon _ Dominique Perrault architecte / Adagp

architects
Dominique Perrault

type
sport

construction
2018

72. Albert Kahn Museum and Garden

2 Rue du Port
92100 Boulogne-Billancourt

Tue - Sun / 11 am - 7 pm
+33 (0)1 40 38 65 66

albert-kahn.hauts-de-seine.fr

 10 > Boulogne
Pont de Saint-Cloud

 260, 6246 > Rhin et
Danube - Musée Albert
Kahn

In the Boulogne-Billancourt area, to the west of the city, is the Albert Kahn Museum and its garden. The museum houses part of his extremely rich collection of over 72,000 photographs, taken in 50 different countries all over the world, the result of a project commissioned by the French banker and philanthropist between 1909 and 1931. Between 2015 and 2022, the Japanese architectural firm of Kengo Kuma was commissioned to design a new 2,300 square metre building as well as the restoration of other nine buildings (eight historical structures and the previous exhibition gallery). The new building is an elongated structure designed to act almost as a filter between Rue du Port and the 9.8 acre park. The external facade is clad in a skin of wood and aluminium slats, creating an imperceptible screen that allows a sense of the structure behind it. The inspiration for this building comes from traditional Japanese architecture, and more specifically, it is derived from the role of the *engawa* which, in the words of the architect, "is not a barrier, or a boundary, but rather a transition between inside and out. An intermediate connective area that allows the building to establish a relationship with its surroundings".

© Kengo Kuma & Associates

architects
Kengo Kuma & Associates

type
cultural

construction
2022

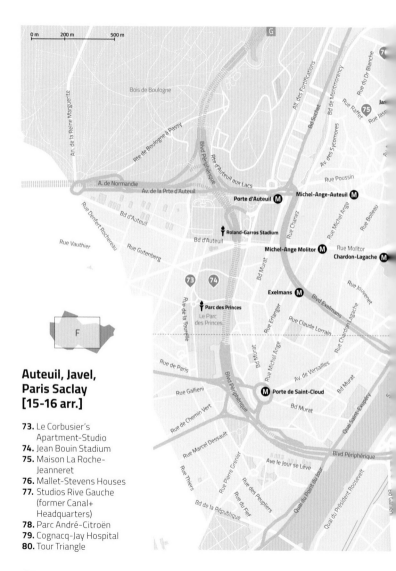

0 m   200 m   500 m

Bois de Boulogne

An. de la Reine Marguerite

Prte de Boulogne à Passy

A. de Normandie

Av. de la Prte d'Auteuil

Rue Denfert-Rochereau

Bd d'Auteuil

Rue Vauthier

Rue Gutenberg

Blvd Périphérique

Prte d'Auteuil aux Lacs

Porte d'Auteuil Ⓜ

Michel-Ange-Auteuil Ⓜ

Rue Poussin

Rue Chanez

Rr de l'Or Blanche

Rue du Dr Blanche

Rue Raffet

Bd Suchet

Bd de Montmorency

Av. des Sycomores

Ⓖ

⑦

Jas

㊄

Rue Jas

Roland-Garros Stadium

Bd d'Auteuil

Michel-Ange Molitor Ⓜ

Rue Molitor

Chardon-Lagache Ⓜ

Rue Michel Ange

Rue Boileau

Bd Murat

㊳ ㊴

Parc des Princes

Le Parc des Princes

Rue de la Tourelle

Exelmans Ⓜ

Blvd Exelmans

Rue Claude Lorrain

Rue Chardon-Lagache

Rue Jouvenet

F

Rue de Paris

Rue Gallieni

Rue de Chemin Vert

Bd Murat

Rue Michel Ange

Porte de Saint-Cloud Ⓜ

Av. de Versailles

Bd Murat

Bd Murat

Blvd Périphérique

Quai Saint-Exupéry

Rue Marcel Dessault

Rue Thiers

Rue Pierre Grenier

Rue des Peupliers

Rue du Fier

Bd de la République

Ave le Jour se Lève

Blvd Périphérique

Quai du Point du Jour

Quai du Président Roosevelt

Bd Caillen

Auteuil, Javel, Paris Saclay [15-16 arr.]

73. Le Corbusier's Apartment-Studio
74. Jean Bouin Stadium
75. Maison La Roche-Jeanneret
76. Mallet-Stevens Houses
77. Studios Rive Gauche (former Canal+ Headquarters)
78. Parc André-Citroën
79. Cognacq-Jay Hospital
80. Tour Triangle

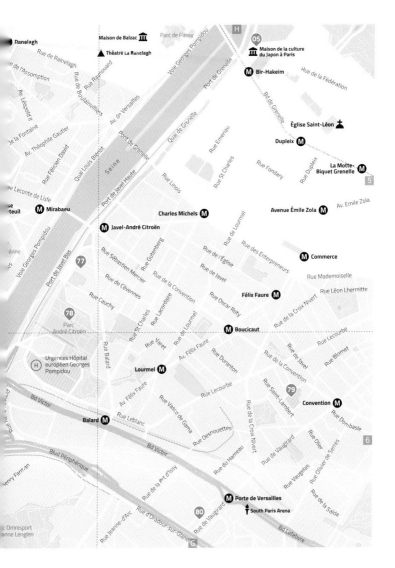

Ranelagh

Maison de Balzac 🏛

Parc de Passy

▲ Théâtre La Ranelagh

Rue de Rainelagh

05

🏛 Maison de la culture du Japon à Paris

Rue de l'Assomption

Ⓜ Bir-Hakeim

Rue de la Fédération

Av. Léopold II

Rue Raynouard

Voie Georges Pompidou

Rue de Boulainvilliers

Port de Grenelle

Bd de Grenelle

de la Fontaine

Av. de Versailles

Quai de Grenelle

Église Saint-Léon ♰

Av. Théophile Gautier

Port de Grenelle

Seine

Rue Emeriau

Dupleix Ⓜ

Rue Félicien David

Quai Louis Blériot

Rue St. Charles

Rue Fondary

Rue Dupleix

La Motte-Biquet Grenelle Ⓜ

Rue Leconte de Lisle

Port de Javel Haute

Rue Linois

5

teuil

Ⓜ Mirabaeu

Charles Michels Ⓜ

Rue de Lourmel

Avenue Émile Zola Ⓜ

Av. Emile Zola

érine

Voie Georges Pompidou

Ⓜ Javel-André Citroën

Rue Sébastien Mercier

Rue Gutenberg

Rue de l'Église

Rue des Entrepreneurs

Ⓜ Commerce

Port de Javel Bas

77

Rue de Cévennes

Rue de Javel

Rue Mademoiselle

Rue de la Convention

Rue Cauchy

Félix Faure Ⓜ

Rue Oscar Roty

Rue Léon Lhermitte

78

Rue St Charles

Rue Lacordaire

Rue de la Croix Nivert

Parc André Citroën

Rue de Lourmel

Ⓜ Boucicaut

Rue de Javel

Rue Lecourbe

Ⓗ Urgences Hôpital européen Georges Pompidou

Rue Varet

Av. Félix Faure

Rue Duranton

Rue de la Convention

Rue Blomet

Rue Balard

Lourmel Ⓜ

Rue Lecourbe

79

Rue Saint-Lambert

Convention Ⓜ

Rue Dombasle

Bd Victor

Balard Ⓜ

Rue Leblanc

Rue Vasco de Gama

Rue Desnouettes

Rue de Vaugirard

Rue Olier

Rue Olivier de Serres

6

Blvd Périphérique

Bd Victor

Rue du Hameau

Rue de la Croix Nivert

Rue Vaugelas

Rue de la Saïda

enry Farman

Rue de la Pte d'Issy

80

Porte de Versailles Ⓜ

♟ South Paris Arena

c Omnisport anne Lenglen

Rue Jeanne-d'Arc

Rue d'Oradour-sur-Glane

Rue de Vaugirard

Bd Lefebvre

G

73. Le Corbusier's Apartment-Studio

24 Rue Nungesser et Coli
75016 Paris

Mon, Tue, Fri / 2 pm - 6 pm
Sat / 10 am - 1 pm,
1.30 pm - 6 pm
+33 (0)1 42 88 75 72
reservation@
fondationlecorbusier.fr
www.fondationlecorbusier.fr

 9 > Exelmans

 52, 72 > La Tourelle

Classified as a historical monument in 1972, the residence and art studio of one of the pioneers of the Modernist architectural movement, is located in the Molitor apartment block on the edge of the Bois de Boulogne. It was designed by Le Corbusier and Pierre Jeanneret between 1931 and 1934. The top two floors of the building, connected by a private elevator, cover a surface of 240 square metres, and include Le Corbusier's personal Parisian residence as well as his art studio. He lived here between 1934, the year of construction, until his death in 1965. The studio was located on the eastern side, while his private residence occupied the western side. The furnishings, and especially the kitchen, were designed in collaboration with Charlotte Perriand. The eighth floor was reserved as a guest suite and provided access to the roof terrace.

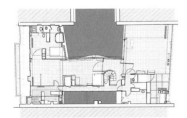

© Valentina S.

architects
Le Corbusier

type
cultural

construction
1934

74. Jean Bouin Stadium

**20-40 Avenue
du Général Sarrail**
75016 Paris

open to the public
+33 (0)1 46 51 00 75

www.stade.fr/stade-jean-bouin

 9 > Exelmans

 52, 72 > La Tourelle

The original stadium was built in 1925 and named after the athlete Jean Bouin, silver medal winner in the 5,000 metres at the 1912 Olympic games. It was first restored in 1970, but required further renovation and upgrading to modern sports standards and regulations; the project was designed by architect Rudy Ricciotti, and completed in 2013. Previously used only for rugby, it now hosts football matches as well, with a seating capacity that was increased from 9,000 in 1970, to 20,000 in 2013. The fundamental feature of the project was the 23,000 square metre external structure that envelopes the stadium. The 3,600 triangular concrete panels create variable geometrical forms to create the two vast external asymmetrical curves. A lightweight, porous mesh effect creates a play of light and shadow. The ground floor, enclosed by metal mesh and glass fixtures, is almost transparent, to permit a continuous effect with the plaza outside. In the words of the architect, Ricciotti: "The mesh wraps around the main body and embraces the shape that is not inspired, but revealed, like the famous photo by Man Ray, where a naked body wrapped in translucent fabric unveils legitimate erotism". The threshold space between the main structure and the external skin is used to house bathroom services, small office spaces, stairs and elevators.

architects
Rudy Ricciotti

type
sport

construction
2013

75. Maison La Roche-Jeanneret

10 Square du Docteur Blanche
75016 Paris

Mon / 1.30 pm - 6 pm
Tue - Fri / 10 am - 12.30 pm,
1.30 pm - 6 pm
Sat / 10 am - 6 pm
+33 (0)1 42 88 75 72
reservation@
fondationlecorbusier.fr
www.fondationlecorbusier.fr

 9 > Jasmin

 22 > Jasmin

Built between 1923 and 1925 these two private, adjoining residences in Rue du Docteur Blanche were the third Parisian commission for Le Corbusier and Pierre Jeanneret. The two houses were designed for the Swiss banker, Raoul La Roche, and for Le Corbusier's brother, the musician Albert Jeanneret. This project is considered a manifesto of the design principles of one of the pioneers of the Modernist architectural movement, which were present in all his early works, but which he then formalised in 1928: free ground plan, free facade design, the pilotis, horizontal ribbon windows, and the roof garden. Today, the Maison Jeanneret is home to the Fondation Le Corbusier in Paris, and the Maison La Roche has become a museum space dedicated to Le Corbusier. It houses the largest collection of his sketches, drawings and projects in the world.

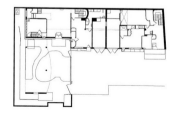

architects
Le Corbusier

type
cultural

construction
1925

76. Mallet-Stevens Houses

Rue Mallet-Stevens
75016 Paris

external viewing only

 9 > Jasmin, Ranelagh

 22 > Jasmin
32 > Raffet

In a location practically unique in Paris, the buildings in Rue Mallet-Stevens represent an urban project, rare for its formal and expressive coherence. Designed by the architect Robert Mallet-Stevens, the complex is located in a private street, and embodies an experiment in the design of a private residential project, using the lexicon and styles of the Modernist movement in a concise and refined manner, without ever becoming conventional. The project arose from the fortuitous meeting in 1924, between the architect and Daniel Dreyfus, the banker and financier. Dreyfus wanted to build a residential complex in the 16th arrondissement, on a 3,800 square metre plot that he owned, a short distance from his home in Rue de l'Assomption. Mallet-Stevens designed a coherent complex of five residential buildings; among these, was a particularly interesting project, the home and art studio of Joël and Jan Martel, two sculptors linked with Art Deco and Cubism. The Hôtel Martel (1926-27) stands out as the most experimental and complex of the various buildings. Visible from the street, in the upper section, the cylindrical staircase acts as the central fulcrum for the distribution of the different levels.

architects
Robert Mallet-Stevens

type
residential

construction
1927

77. Studios Rive Gauche (ex Canal+ Headquarters)

2 Rue des Cévennes
75015 Paris

partly open to the public

 10 > Javel - André Citroën

 RER C > Javel

 30 > Javel
30, 88 > Cauchy

The headquarters of the French production company, Studios Rive Gauche, are located inside an L-shaped building composed of two blocks situated along Quai André Citroën and Rue des Cévennes. When it was inaugurated in 1992, the building was home to Canal+, a French television channel, transferred a few years later to the Paris suburb of Issy-les-Moulineaux. The main entrance features a large cantilevered projecting shelter. Inside, positioned between the two buildings, a vast three-storey high foyer welcomes visitors and is also used as a pedestrian walkway through to the park at the rear. The shell is composed of white enamelled steel panels. Terraces, horizontal sun screens and vertical brises-soleil enhance the external facades facing both the street and the park. The entirely glazed, curved segment of the north-west facade was designed as a monumental "urban window". The production studios, some underground, are arranged on four floors, while at the rear of the two corner buildings, the restaurant and meeting rooms overlook a square garden. The project summarises the distinctive style of the American architect, Richard Meier: immaculate white surfaces, modular composition, and constant flexibility.

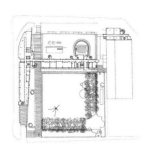

© Giacomo Carpina

architects
Richard Meier and Partners

type
administrative

construction
1992

78. Parc André-Citroën

2 Rue Cauchy
75015 Paris

open to the public

 11 > Javel - André
Citroën

 RER C > Javel

 30, 88 > Parc
André Citroën
42, 88, 169 >
Hôpital Européen
Georges Pompidou

This park was the site of the former Citroën automobile production plant until the 1970s. The 35 acre area was redeveloped in the mid 1980s as part of an urban plan to create a large public park for relaxation and entertainment in the city centre, and was named Parc André-Citroën. Inaugurated in 1992, the project was the result of a competition won by the team led by architect Patrick Berger and landscape designer and agronomist Gilles Clément. The park is based on the concept of nature in the city. Observing the elements that compose the layout of this public space, the horizontal aspect is very evident: a vast rectangular green lawn is crossed diagonally by a wide path. Underlining the rational composition of the design, water courses and paved routes respect the clean geometry of the overall layout, also defined by the structural rhythm of a series of six smaller gardens, each one unique for its different planted shrub species.

©.EQRoy / shutterstock.com

architects
Patrick Berger, Gilles Clément

type
public space

construction
1992

79. Cognacq-Jay Hospital

15 Rue Eugène Millon
75015 Paris

partly open to the public
+33 (0)1 45 30 85 00

www.hopital.cognacq-jay.fr

12 > Convention
8 > Boucicaut

39, 62, 80, N13, N62 >
Convention - Lecourbe

As the result of a competition launched in 1999, the redevelopment project for the Cognacq-Jay Hospital in Paris was assigned to the Japanese architectural firm of Toyo Ito and was inaugurated in 2006. The private clinic is mainly composed of two independent buildings, one built along Rue Blomet, and the other, opposite, in Rue Eugène-Millon. The two main buildings enclose a private garden reserved for the hospital patients and staff. This not only provides a pleasant space to relax, but also grants beautiful views from the hospital rooms. The project is coherent with the style and scale of the residential urban fabric of the 15th arrondissement. The external facades are aligned with those of the surrounding buildings, but clad in a different material. The walls are covered with a glass skin on a metal frame that creates a play between transparent, opaque and translucent effects.

© Toyo Ito & Associates

© Philippe Ruault

architects
Toyo Ito

type
healthcare

construction
2006

80. Tour Triangle

Porte de Versailles
75015 Paris

external viewing only

 12 > Porte de Versailles
8 > Balard

 54, 80 > Porte
de Versailles -
Boulevard Lefebvre
54 > Porte de Versailles
- Boulevard Lefebvre

 T2 > Porte de Versailles
T3a > Porte de
Versailles - Parc
des Expositions

The Triangle will be the third highest building in Paris after the Eiffel Tower and the Tour Montparnasse. The slim glass blade structure, designed by Swiss architects Herzog & de Meuron, will rise in the Porte de Versailles quarter, near the Paris Expo Exhibition Centre. It will be built in the historic axis of Rue de Vaugirard and Avenue Ernest Renan reconnecting Paris to Issy-les-Moulineaux. Despite controversy because of the building's soaring height, Triangle will be completed in 2026, making a striking impact on the Paris skyline. The pyramid shape was designed to reduce the amount and duration of shade generated on the surrounding buildings. The northern side has a tiered step formation and the building is powered by solar and geothermal energy with a highly efficient envelope. The architect Jacques Herzog stated that the tower was designed as a "vertical city" in other words, a rather very mix used destination that offers many services to the city. The building will indeed house a hotel, retail stores, a business centre, a nursery, cultural spaces, co-working offices, a medical center and a large bike park of approximately 2,000 square metres. It is designed to be open to the public; panoramic elevators will take visitors to the summit of the building where a large terrace and restaurant will offer exclusive and extraordinary views of the city.

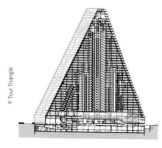

© Tour Triangle

architects
Herzog & de Meuron

type
multi-purpose

construction
ongoing

81. Paris-Saclay

91120 Palaiseau,
91400 Orsay,
91190 Gif-sur-Yvette

partly open to the public

18 > Palaiseau, Orsay-
Gif (under construction)

14, 91-06, 91-10,
N63 > Polytechnique
Lozère, Ferme de
La Vauve
91-06, 91-08, 91-10
> Palaiseau - Campus,
Université Paris-Saclay
7, 11 > De Broglie
9 > Moulon
11 > Centralesupélec

Today the Campus Urbain, part of the Paris-Saclay cluster still under construction, includes schools, universities, student residences, businesses, and is part of a vast masterplan designed by Michel Desvigne with the Xaveer De Geyter and Floris Alkemade architectural firms – and aimed at interaction between urban and rural areas. In a territory rich in farms, wetlands and woods, the urban islands composed of existing buildings and new architectural complexes are connected through the landscape and expanded infrastructures, including the future Metro line 18. The route through the campus begins at Palaiseau, in the area where the initial École Polytechnique nucleus was built. Inside this same perimeter, enclosed by the Boulevard des Maréchaux, CAB Architectes created the ENSAE ParisTech university building. The project drew its inspiration from the environmental context: views of the woods motivated the architects to erect a light structure set on the terrain, with unrestricted views from the facade overlooking the woods to provide direct contact. On the other hand, the nearby Institut Mines-Télécom by Grafton Architects was designed to bring the vegetation and public space inside the complex, by constructing on the boundary of the available area to obtain spacious internal courtyards. A short distance away, Résidence Rosalind Franklin, designed by the Bruther and Baukunst firms, provides 192 student apartments, parking, communal spaces and shops; it is based on a U-shaped plan with a central garden, and an almost totally glazed ground floor, so that it appears to be in visual and physical continuation with the exterior. Moving across the campus towards the west, is the geographical heart of the hub with a view of the monumental Institut des Sciences Moléculaires d'Orsay – ISMO. For this building, the Dutch architects, KAAN Architecten proposed a scheme integrating construction and urban space: the entrance is located below street level, and can be reached by a ramp or steps along the west side of the building. Further north, along Avenue

architects
Michel Desvigne,
Xaveer De Geyter Architects,
Floris Alkemade (masterplan)

type
multi-purpose

construction
ongoing

91120 Palaiseau,
91400 Orsay,
91190 Gif-sur-Yvette

partly open to the public

18 > Palaiseau, Orsay-Gif (under construction)

14, 91-06, 91-10, N63 > Polytechnique Lozère, Ferme de La Vauve
91-06, 91-08, 91-10 > Palaiseau - Campus, Université Paris-Saclay
7, 11 > De Broglie
9 > Moulon
11 > Centralesupélec

des Sciences is the recently built Centre Henri Moissan – Pôle Biologie, Pharmacie, Chimie, the work of Bernard Tschumi and Group 6, located opposite the future Orsay-Gif Metro station. In Rue Juliot Curie, parallel to this avenue, is Public by the Muoto firm; it is one of the numerous multi-purpose buildings in this area. It houses a cafeteria, a university restaurant, communal spaces, fitness centre and open-air playing fields, arranged in a step formation to provide every level with a panoramic view of the plateau landscape. Continuing along this street are the buildings and open spaces surrounding the Parc du Moulon. The first building is Francis Bouygues – École CentraleSupélec, designed by the Gigon-Guyer firm and conceived as a "Building-town", arranged in a grid network of streets and plazas. Additional urban value is created by the OMA project, the nearby Lab City CentraleSupélec, with the construction of a street that cuts a diagonal passage through the buildings, based on a grid system, creating an ideal connection between interior and exterior. To the west of the park the LAN and CVA firms worked with Topotek 1 to create a campus and a series of buildings with 900 student residences, able to house 1,082 students. The central cylindrical structures, the "Muses", are decorated with photo engraved figures from Greek mythology. A small pedestrian area, an extension of Parc du Moulon, leads to the École Normale Supérieure designed by Renzo Piano Building Workshop. The building includes an internal garden with trees to reduce the effect of the winds from the Saclay plateau which is particularly exposed; the terraces and the garden itself facilitate rain water runoff, despite the lack of drainage caused by the clay soil. In this way the project manages to transform certain natural environmental problems into a significant resource. The Campus Urbain is the largest European urban project currently under construction; by 2030 it will house 20,000 research and teaching staff, 30,000 students, 20,000 employees, and about 15,000 residents.

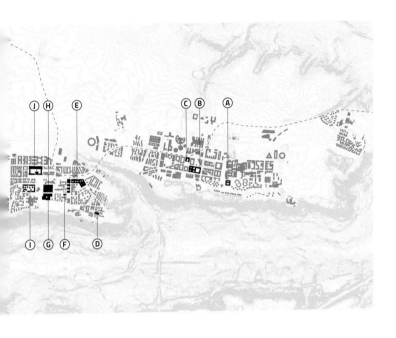

A. **ENSAE ParisTech**
   CAB Architectes (2017)
B. **Istituto Mines-Télécom**
   Grafton Architects
   (2019)
C. **Résidence**
   Rosalind Franklin
   Bruther, Baukunst
   (2020)
D. **Institut des Sciences**
   Moléculaires d'Orsay –
   ISMO
   KAAN Architecten (2018)

E. **Centre Henri Moissan –**
   Pôle Biologie,
   Pharmacie, Chimie
   Bernard Tschumi,
   Group 6 (2023)
F. **Public Condenser**
   Muoto (2016)
G. **Francis Bouygues –**
   École CentraleSupélec
   Gigon-Guyer (2017)
H. **Lab City**
   CentraleSupélec
   OMA (2017)

I. **900 student residences**
   LAN, CVA, 1oputek 1
   (2018)
J. **École Normale**
   Supérieure
   Renzo Piano Building
   Workshop (2020)

Olympic and Paralympic venues

A1. La Concorde
A2. Grand Palais
A3. Alexandre III Bridge
A4. Invalides
A5. Trocadéro
A6. Eiffel Tower Stadium
A7. Champ de Mars Arena
A8. Hôtel de Ville
B1. Bercy Arena
C1. Vaires-sur-Marne Nautical Stadium
C2. Clichy-sous-Bois
C3. North Paris Arena
C4. Le Bourget Sport climbing venue
C5. La Courneuve
C6. Stade de France
C7. Porte de la Chapelle Arena
D1. Aquatics Centre
D2. Yves-du-Manoir Stadium
E1. Paris La Défense Arena in Nanterre
F1. Roland-Garros Stadium
F2. Parc des Princes
F3. South Paris Arena
F4. Château de Versailles
F5. Saint-Quentin-en-Yvelines Velodrome
F6. Saint-Quentin-en-Yvelines BMX Stadium
F7. Elancourt Hill
F8. National Golf

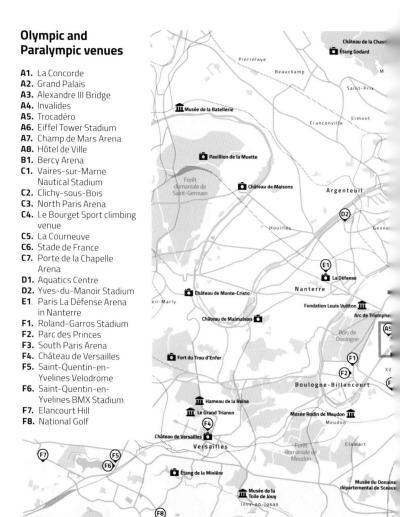

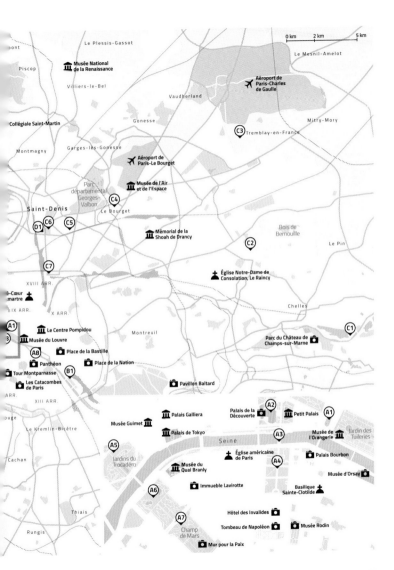

Le Plessis-Gassot

Le Mesnil-Amelot

0 km   2 km   5 km

ont

Piscop

🏛 Musée National
de la Renaissance

Villiers-le-Bel

✈ Aéroport de
Paris-Charles
de Gaulle

Vaudherland

Collégiale Saint-Martin

Gonesse

Mitry-Mory

Ⓒ3 Tremblay-en-France

Montmagny

Garges-lès-Gonesse

✈ Aéroport de
Paris-Le Bourget

🏛 Musée de l'Air
et de l'Espace

Parc
départemental
Georges-
Valbon

Ⓒ4

Le Bourget

Saint-Denis Ⓒ6 Ⓒ5

Ⓓ1

🏛 Mémorial de la
Shoah de Drancy

Ⓒ2

Bois de
Bernouille

Le Pin

Ⓒ7

XVIII ARR.

-Cœur
martre ✝

SIX ARR.

X ARR.

✝ Église Notre-Dame de
Consolation, Le Raincy

Chelles

Ⓐ1
3

🏛 Le Centre Pompidou
🏛 Musée du Louvre

Ⓐ8 📷 Place de la Bastille

📷 Panthéon

📷 Tour Montparnasse
📷 Les Catacombes
de Paris

Ⓑ1

Montreuil

📷 Place de la Nation

📷 Pavillon Baltard

Ⓒ1

Parc du Château de
Champs-sur-Marne 📷

ARR.

XIII ARR.

ouge

Le Kremlin-Bicêtre

Ⓐ5

Musée Guimet 🏛

Jardins du
Trocadéro

🏛 Palais Galliera

🏛 Palais de Tokyo

Palais de la
Découverte 📷 Ⓐ2

Ⓐ3

Seine

🏛 Petit Palais Ⓐ1

🏛 Musée de
l'Orangerie

Jardin des
Tuileries

Cachan

✝ Église américaine
de Paris

Ⓐ4

📷 Palais Bourbon

Musée d'Orsay 📷

🏛 Musée du
Quai Branly

Ⓐ6

📷 Immeuble Lavirotte

Basilique ✝
Sainte-Clotilde

Thiais

Ⓐ7

Champ
de Mars

Hôtel des Invalides 📷

Tombeau de Napoléon 📷   📷 Musée Rodin

Rungis

📷 Mur pour la Paix

211

Museums

Cité des sciences et de l'industrie
Exhibition Centre dedicated to Science
-
30 Avenue Corentin Cariou, 75019 Paris

www.cite-sciences.fr
infocontact(at)cite-sciences.fr
+33 (0)1 85 53 99 74

Conciergerie
Medieval Royal Palace
-
2 Boulevard du Palais, 75001 Paris

www.paris-conciergerie.fr
+33 (0)1 53 40 60 80

Dalí Paris
Permanent collection of works by Salvador Dalí
-
11 Rue Poulbot, 75018 Paris

www.daliparis.com
+33 (0)1 42 64 40 10

Fluctuart – Centre d'art urbain
Urban Art Centre
-
2 Port du Gros Caillou, 75007 Paris

fluctuart.fr
reservation@fluctuart.fr
+33 7 67 02 44 37

Grand Palais
Exhibition pavilion and events centre
-
3 Avenue du Général Eisenhower, 75008 Paris

www.grandpalais.fr
dpo@rmngp.fr
+33 (0)1 40 13 48 00

MAM Musée d'Art Moderne de Paris
Museum of Modern and Contemporary Art
-
11 Avenue du Président Wilson, 75116 Paris

www.mam.paris.fr
+33 (0)1 53 67 40 00

Musée de l'Orangerie
Museum of Impressionism and
Post Impressionism paintings
-
Jardin Tuileries, 75001 Paris

www.musee-orangerie.fr
information@musee-orangerie.fr
+33 (0)1 44 50 43 00

Musée du Louvre
Museum of ancient and modern art
-
Rue de Rivoli, 75001 Paris

www.louvre.fr
info@louvre.fr
+33 (0)1 40 20 53 17

Musée Guimet
Museum of Asian art
-
6 Place d'Iéna, 75116 Paris

www.guimet.fr
contact@guimet.fr
+33 (0)1 56 52 54 33

Musée national Picasso-Paris
Public collection of works by Picasso
-
5 Rue de Thorigny, 75003 Paris

www.museepicassoparis.fr
contact@museepicassoparis.fr
+33 (0)1 85 56 00 36

Musée Rodin
Art museum dedicated
to works by Auguste Rodin
-
77 Rue de Varenne, 75007 Paris

www.musee-rodin.fr
resagroupescite@universcience.fr
+33 (0)1 44 18 61 10

Museo Grévin
Wax works museum
-
10 Boulevard Montmartre, 75009 Paris

www.grevin-paris.com
contact@grevin.com
+33 (0)1 47 70 85 05

Petit Palais
Exhibition pavilion with permanent art collection
-
Avenue Winston Churchill, 75008 Paris

+33 (0)1 53 43 40 00

Theatres

Bobino
14-20 Rue de la Gaîté, 75014 Paris

bobino.fr
billetterie@bobino.fr
+33 (0)1 43 27 24 24

Comédie-Française
1 Place Colette, 75001 Paris

www.comedie-francaise.fr
+33 825 10 16 80

Folies Bergère
32 Rue Richer, 75009 Paris

www.foliesbergere.com
+33 800 00 16 50

L'Olympia
28 Boulevard des Capucines, 75009 Paris

www.olympiahall.com
+33 (0)1 47 42 94 88

Opéra Bastille
Place de la Bastille, 75012 Paris

www.operadeparis.fr
accessibilité@operadeparis.fr
+33 (0)1 71 25 24 23

Opéra Garnier
Place de l'Opéra, 75009 Paris

www.operadeparis.fren
accessibilité@operadeparis.fr
+33 (0)1 40 01 18 50

Théâtre de la Ville
2 Place du Châtelet, 75004 Paris

www.theatredelaville-paris.com
+33 (0)1 42 74 22 77

Théâtre des Bouffes du Nord
37 bis Boulevard de la Chapelle, 75010 Paris

www.bouffesdunord.com
+33 (0)1 46 07 34 50

Théâtre des Bouffes-Parisiens
4 Rue Monsigny, 75002 Paris

www.bouffesparisiens.com
reservation@bouffesparisiens.com
+33 (0)1 42 96 92 42

Théâtre des Champs-Élysées
15 Avenue Montaigne, 75008 Paris

www.theatrechampselysees.fr
contact@theatrechampselysees.fr
+33 (0)1 49 52 50 50

Théâtre du Palais-Royal
38 Rue de Montpensier, Paris

theatrepalaisroyal.com
tpr@theatrepalaisroyal.com
+33 (0)1 42 97 40 00

Théâtre du Rond-Point
2bis Av Franklin D. Roosevelt, 75008 Paris

www.theatredurondpoint.fr
+33 (0)1 44 95 98 21

Théâtre Marigny
Carré Marigny, 75008 Paris

www.theatremarigny.fr
billetterie@theatremarigny.fr
+33 (0)1 76 49 47 12

Théâtre Mogador
25 Rue de Mogador, 75009 Paris

www.theatremogador.com
+33 (0)1 53 33 45 30

Hotels

Hôtel Audran • •
7 Rue Audran, 75018 Paris

hotelaudran.com
contact@hotelaudran.com
+33 (0)1 42 58 79 59

• • • expensive
• • mid-range
• inexpensive

Hôtel Beauséjour • •
71 Avenue Parmentier, 75011 Paris

www.hotelbeausejourparis.com
reservation@hotelbeausejourparis.com
+33 (0)1 47 00 38 16

Juliana Hôtel Paris • • •
10-12 Rue Cognacq Jay, 75007 Paris

www.hoteljuliana.paris
contact@guide.paris
+33 (0)1 44 05 70 00

Hôtel Lancaster Paris Champs-Élysées • • •
7 Rue de Berri, 75008 Paris

www.hotel-lancaster.com
concierge@hotel-lancaster.fr
+33 (0)1 40 76 40 76

Hôtel Le Twelve • •
82 Avenue du Docteur Arnold Netter,
75012 Paris

www.hotel-twelve.com
contact@hotel-twelve.com
+33 (0)1 43 43 78 50

Hôtel Lutetia • • •
45 Boulevard Raspail, 75006 Paris

www.hotellutetia.com
contact@hotellutetia.com
+33 (0)1 49 54 46 00

Hôtel Montaigne • • •
6 Avenue Montaigne, 75008 Paris

montaigne-hotel.com
resa@montaigne-hotel.com
+33 (0)1 80 97 40 00

Hôtel Paris Villette • •
56 Rue Curial, 75019 Paris

www.parisvillette.com
hotel@parisvillette.com
+33 (0)1 40 37 50 74

Hôtel Paris Voltaire • •
79 Rue Sedaine, 75011 Paris

www.hotel-paris-voltaire.fr
hotel-paris-voltaire@hotmail.fr
+33 (0)1 48 05 44 66

Hôtel Parister • • •
19 Rue Saulnier, 75009 Paris

www.hotelparister.com
bonjour@hotelparister.com
+33 (0)1 80 50 91 91

Le Cinq Codet • • •
5 Rue Louis Codet, 7500 Paris

lecinqcodet.com
contact@le5codet.com
+33 (0)1 53 85 15 60

Le Damantin Hôtel & Spa • • •
1 Rue Bayard, 75008 Paris

www.ledamantin.com
contact@ledamantin.com
+33 (0)1 53 75 62 62

Le Pavillon de la Reine – Hôtel & Spa • • •
28 Place des Vosges, 75003 Paris

www.pavillon-de-la-reine.com
contact@pdlr.fr
+33 (0)1 40 29 19 19

Restaurants

Grand Café Capucines • • •
4 Boulevard des Capucines, 75009 Paris

www.legrandcafe.com
+33 (0)1 43 12 19 00

• • • expensive
• • mid-range
• inexpensive

Brasserie Mollard • • •
115 Rue Saint-Lazare, 75008 Paris

www.mollard.fr
espace.clients@mollard.fr
+33 (0)1 43 87 50 22

La Grange aux Loups • • •
8 Rue du 11 Novembre, 60300 Paris

www.lagrangeauxloups.com
contact@lagrangeauxloups.com
+33 (0)3 44 25 33 79

Le Taillevent • • •
15 Rue Lamennais, 75008 Paris

taillevent.com
contact@taillevent.com
+33 (0)1 44 95 15 00

La Tour d'Argent • • •
15 Quai de la Tournelle, 75005 Paris

tourdargent.com
resa@tourdargent.com
+33 (0)1 43 54 23 31

Le Gabriel • • •
42 Avenue Gabriel, 75008 Paris

www.lareserve-paris.com
reservations@lareserve-paris.com
+33 (0)1 58 36 60 60

Le Train Bleu • •
Gare de Lyon, Place Louis Armand, 75012 Paris

www.le-train-bleu.com
+33 (0)1 43 43 09 06

Le Petit Vendôme • •
8 Rue des Capucines, 75002 Paris

lepetitvendome.fr
+33 (0)1 42 61 05 88

Allard • •
41 Rue Saint-André des Arts, 75006 Paris

www.restaurant-allard.fr
restaurant.allard@ducasse-paris.com
+33 (0)1 43 26 48 23

Racines • •
8 Passage des Panoramas, 75002 Paris

racinesparis.com
contact@racinesparis.com
+33 (0)1 40 13 06 41

Foyer de la Madeleine •
Place de la Madeleine, 75008 Paris

www.foyerdelamadeleine.fr
foyerdelamadeleine@orange.fr
+33 (0)1 47 42 39 84

Breizh Café •
1 Rue de l'Odéon, 75006 Paris

breizhcafe.com
+33 (0)1 42 72 13 77

Architectural offices

2P Architectes & Associés
38 Rue La Bruyère, 75009 Paris

www.2portzamparc.com
contact@2Parchitectes.com
+33 (0)1 80 05 32 00

Atelier de l'île
89 Rue du Fb. Saint-Antoine, 75011 Paris

www.atile.fr
paris@atile.fr
+ 33 (0)1 48 06 22 00

Ateliers Jean Nouvel
10 Cité d'Angoulême, 75011 Paris

www.jeannouvel.com
info@jeannouvel.fr
+33 (0)1 49 23 83 83

Bernard Tschumi Architects
188 Boulevard Saint-Germain, 75007 Paris

www.tschumi.com
press@tschumi.com
+33 (0)1 53 01 90 70

BRUTHER
3 bis Rue Pelleport, 75020 Paris

bruther.biz
contact@bruther.biz
+33 (0)1 45 35 58 96

CAB Architectes
55 Rue Pixérécourt, 75020 Paris

www.cabarchitectes.com
+33 (0)1 44 83 02 13

Chatillon Architectes
61 Rue de Dunkerque, 75009 Paris

www.chatillonarchitectes.com
contact@chatillonarchitectes.com
+ 33 (0)1 48 78 31 52

Dietmar Feichtinger Architects
80 Rue Edouard Vaillant, 93100 Montreuil

feichtingerarchitects.com
paris@feichtingerarchitects.com
+33 (0)1 43 71 15 22

Dominique Perrault Architecture
6 Rue Bouvier, 75011 Paris

www.perraultarchitecture.com
dpa@perraultarchitecture.com
+33 (0)1 44 06 00 00

Experience
29 Rue des Trois-Bornes, 75011 Paris

www.experienceparis.eu
office@experienceparis.eu
+33 (0)1 40 18 40 65

Frédéric Druot Architecture
14 Avenue de l'Opéra, 75001 Paris

www.druot.net
info@druot.net
+33 (0)1 47 03 47 44

Studio Fuksas
85 Rue du Temple, 75003 Paris

fuksas.com
secretariat@fuksas.com
+33 (0)1 44 61 83 83

Herzog & de Meuron
72 Rue des Archives, 75003 Paris

www.herzogdemeuron.com
info@herzogdemeuron.com
+33 (0)1 76 21 25 30

Jouin Manku
2 Rue Paul Cézanne, 75008 Paris

www.jouinmanku.com
agence@jouinmanku.com
+33 (0)1 55 28 89 20

KAAN Architecten
8 Rue Saint-Merri, 75004 Paris

kaanarchitecten.com
+33 (0)1 81 69 55 55

Kuma & Associates Europe
104 Rue Oberkampf, 75011 Paris

kkaa.co.jp
KUMA@kkaa.eu
+33 (0)1 44 88 94 94

Lacaton & Vassal Architectes
80 Rue de Paris, 93100 Montreuil

www.lacatonvassal.com
mail@lacatonvassal.com
+33 (0)1 47 23 49 09

LAN
47 Rue Popincourt, 75011 Paris

www.lan-paris.com
info@lan-paris.com
+33 (0)1 43 70 00 60

MAARU
30 Allée Vivaldi, 75012 Paris

maaru.fr
contact@maaru.fr

Muoto architecture studio
48 Avenue Claude Vellefaux, 75010 Paris

www.studiomuoto.com
info@studiomuoto.com
+33 (0)9 54 81 09 00

MVRDV
49 Boulevard de la Villette, 75010 Paris

www.mvrdv.com
office@mvrdv.com
+33 (0)1 85 73 48 24

Nicolas Hugoo Architecture
142 Rue du Faubourg Saint Denis, 75010 Paris

nicolashugoo.fr
contact@nicolashugoo.fr
+33 (0)1 84 17 75 39

Patrick Berger architecte
14 Rue Bertin Poirée, 75001 Paris

patrickberger.fr

PÉRIPHÉRIQUES MARIN + TROTTIN Architectes
8 Rue Montcalm, 75018 Paris

www.marin-trottin.com
contact@marin-trottin.com
+33 (0)1 44 92 05 01

Perrot & Richard Architectes
60 Rue Saint-André-des-Arts, 75006 Paris

www.perrot-richard.com
contact@perrot-richard.com
+33 (0)1 53 30 00 80

Renzo Piano Building Workshop
34 Rue des Archives, 75004 Paris

www.rpbw.com
+33 (0)1 44 61 49 00

RSHP
3 Rue de la Tour d'Auvergne, 75009 Paris

rshp.com
enquiries@rshp.com
+33 (0)1 89 16 88 77

Snøhetta
19 Rue de Cléry, 75002 Paris

www.snohetta.com
studioparis@snohetta.com
+33 (0)1 84 79 78 60

SRA Architectes
26 Avenue de Paris, 92320 Châtillon

sra-architectes.com
agence@sra-architectes.com
+33 (0)1 46 55 99 11

Index by architect

Adolf Loos	Tristan Tzara House / 53 (p. 144)
Atelier de l'île	Cinémathèque Française / 35 (p. 102)
Ateliers Jean Nouvel	Musée du Quai Branly / 07 (p. 40); Institut du Monde Arabe / 17 (p. 66); Fondation Cartier pour l'art contemporain / 20 (p. 72); Philharmonie de Paris / 48 (p. 132)
Bernard Bijvoet	Maison de Verre / 02 (p. 30)
Bernard Tschumi	Parc de la Villette / 46 (p. 128)
Borja Huidobro	Ministry of Economics and Finance / 34 (p. 100)
BRUTHER	Residence for Researchers Julie-Victoire Daubié / 24 (p. 80); Cultural and Sports Center Saint-Blaise / 41 (p. 118); Social Housing Pelleport / 42 (p. 120)
Chatillon Architectes	La Piscine des Amiraux / 54 (p. 146); Maison des Sciences de l'Homme (restoration) / 03 (p. 32)
Christian de Portzamparc	Cité de la musique / 47 (p. 130); Paris La Défense Arena / 68 (p. 178)
David Chipperfield Architects	Morland Mixité Capitale / 16 (p. 64)
Dietmar Feichtinger Architects	Passerelle Simone-de-Beauvoir / 36 (p. 104)
Dominique Perrault	National Library of France – François-Mitterrand / 32 (p. 96); The Olympic and Paralympic Village – Paris 2024 Île-Saint-Denis / 57 (p. 152); Longchamp Racecourse / 71 (p. 184)
Émile Aillaud	Tours Aillaud / 70 (p. 182)
Emmanuel Cattani & Associés	Fondation Cartier pour l'art contemporain / 20 (p. 72)
Empreinte	La Défense: Terrasses Boieldieu / 65 (p. 172)
Eugène Beaudouin	Maison du Peuple de Clichy / 58 (p. 154)
Experience	Chris Marker Student Housing / 23 (p. 78)
Floris Alkemade	Paris-Saclay (masterplan) / 81 (p. 206)
Foster + Partners	Apple Store Champs-Élysées / 09 (p. 44)
Franck Hammoutène	Notre Dame de Pentecôte / 66 (p. 174)
Frank Gehry	Cinémathèque Française / 35 (p. 102); Fondation Louis Vuitton / 63 (p. 168)
Frédéric Druot	Tour Bois-le-Prêtre / 59 (p. 156)
Gae Aulenti	Musée d'Orsay / 01 (p. 28)
Gérard Grandval	Les Choux de Créteil / 37 (p. 110)
Gilles Clément	Parc André-Citroën / 78 (p. 200)
Gustafson Porter + Bowman	Site Tour Eiffel / 06 (p. 38)
Harry Seidler	Australian Embassy / 05 (p. 36)
Henri Gaudin	Rue de Ménilmontant Social Housing / 43 (p. 122)
Henri Sauvage	La Piscine des Amiraux / 54 (p. 146)
Herzog & de Meuron	Tour Triangle / 80 (p. 204)
Ieoh Ming Pei	Musée du Louvre (Pyramid) / 10 (p. 46)
Igrec Ingénierie	La Défense: Terrasses Boieldieu / 65 (p. 172)
III-Studio	Pigalle Duperré / 52 (p. 142)
Isabelle Marin	Rue de Ménilmontant Social Housing / 43 (p. 122)
Jean Dubuisson	Maine-Montparnasse II Residential Building / 22 (p. 76)
Jean Prouvé	Maison du Peuple de Clichy / 58 (p. 154)
Jean Renaudie	Les Étoiles d'Ivry / 29 (p. 90)
Johann Otto von Spreckelsen	Grande Arche de La Défense / 67 (p. 176)
Jouin Manku	Maison du Peuple de Clichy (restoration) / 58 (p. 154)
Jumeau + Marin + Trottin / PÉRIPHÉRIQUES ARCHITECTES	Atrium Université Pierre & Marie Curie / 18 (p. 68)

Kengo Kuma & Associates	Saint-Denis Pleyel Railway Station / 56 (p. 150); Albert Kahn Museum and Garden / 72 (p. 186)
L.E.A.	La Défense: Terrasses Boieldieu / 65 (p. 172)
Lacaton & Vassal	Palais de Tokyo – extension / 08 (p. 42); Tour Bois-le-Prêtre / 59 (p. 156)
LAN	40 Housing Units / 61 (p. 160); Student Residence / 51 (p. 138); Torre Wood Up / 30 (p. 92)
Le Corbusier	Swiss Pavilion / 25 (p. 82); Maison du Brésil / 26 (p. 84); Maison Planeix / 28 (p. 88); Cité de Refuge – Salvation Army Hostel / 31 (p. 94); Maison Jaoul / 64 (p. 170); Le Corbusier's Apartment-Studio / 73 (p. 190); Maison La Roche-Jeanneret / 75 (p. 194)
Louis Arretche	Ministry of Economics and Finance / 34 (p. 100)
Lúcio Costa	Maison du Brésil / 26 (p. 84)
MAARU	La Défense: Terrasses Boieldieu / 65 (p. 172)
Manuel Núñez Yanowsky	Les Arènes de Picasso / 38 (p. 112)
Marcel Breuer	Australian Embassy / 05 (p. 36)
Marcel Lods	Maison des Sciences de l'Homme / 03 (p. 32); Maison du Peuple de Clichy / 58 (p. 154)
Mario Bellini	Musée du Louvre (Department of Islamic Arts) / 10 (p. 46)
Martin van Treeck	Les Orgues de Flandre / 50 (p. 136)
Meier and Partners	Studios Rive Gauche (ex Canal+ Headquarters) / 77 (p. 198)
Métra+Associés	Philharmonie de Paris (concert hall) / 48 (p. 132)
Michel Desvigne	Paris-Saclay (masterplan) / 81 (p. 206)
MVRDV	Gaîté Montparnasse / 21 (p. 74); Pushed Slab / 27 (p. 86)
OMA	Fondation d'entreprise Galeries Lafayette / 15 (p. 58)
Oscar Niemeyer	Headquarters of the French Communist Party / 44 (p. 124)
Patrick Berger	Parc André-Citroën / 78 (p. 200)
Paul Chemetov	Ministry of Economics and Finance / 34 (p. 100); Headquarters of the French Communist Party / 44 (p. 124)
Perrot & Richard Architects	Maison du Peuple de Clichy (restoration) / 58 (p. 154)
Pier Luigi Nervi	Australian Embassy / 05 (p. 36)
Pierre Chareau	Maison de Verre / 02 (p. 30)
Pierre Gangnet	La Défense: Terrasses Boieldieu / 65 (p. 172)
Pierre Jeanneret	Swiss Pavilion / 25 (p. 82); Cité de Refuge – Salvation Army Hostel / 31 (p. 94)
Raymond Lopez	Tour Bois-le-Prêtre / 59 (p. 156)
Renée Gailhoustet	Les Étoiles d'Ivry / 29 (p. 90)
Renzo Piano Building Workshop	Atelier Brâncuși / 13 (p. 54); Centre Georges Pompidou / 14 (p. 56); Fondation Jérôme Seydoux Pathé / 19 (p. 70); Rue de Meaux Housing / 45 (p. 126); Paris Courthouse / 60 (p. 158)
Ricardo Bofill Taller de Arquitectura	Espaces d'Abraxas / 39 (p. 114)
Richard Rogers	Centre Georges Pompidou / 14 (p. 56)
Robert Mallet-Stevens	Mallet-Stevens Houses / 76 (p. 196)
Roman Karasinski	Ministry of Economics and Finance / 34 (p. 100)
Rudy Ricciotti	Musée du Louvre (Department of Islamic Arts) / 10 (p. 46); le19M – Fashion Manufactory of Chanel / 49 (p. 134); Jean Bouin Stadium / 74 (p. 192)
SANAA	La Samaritaine / 11 (p. 50); Avenue du Maréchal Fayolle Housing / 62 (p. 166)
Snøhetta	Le Monde Group Headquarters / 33 (p. 98)
SRA Architectes	Le Monde Group Headquarters / 33 (p. 98)
Studio Fuksas	National Archives of France / 55 (p. 148)
Tadao Ando Architect & Associates	Meditation Space UNESCO / 04 (p. 34); Bourse de Commerce – Pinault Collection / 12 (p. 52)

Topotek 1   ZAC Porte de Vincennes / 40 (p. 116); ZAC Le Croissant / 69 (p. 180)
Toyo Ito & Associates   Cognacq-Jay Hospital / 79 (p. 202)
Vladimir Bodiansky   Maison du Peuple de Clichy / 58 (p. 154)
Xaveer De Geyter Architects   Paris-Saclay (masterplan) / 81 (p. 206)

Index by project

40 Housing Units / 61	LAN	160
Albert Kahn Museum and Garden / 72	Kengo Kuma & Associates	186
Apple Store Champs-Élysées / 09	Foster + Partners	44
Atelier Brâncuși / 13	Renzo Piano Building Workshop	54
Atrium Université Pierre & Marie Curie / 18	Jumeau + Marin + Trottin / PÉRIPHÉRIQUES ARCHITECTES	68
Australian Embassy / 05	Harry Seidler, Marcel Breuer, Pier Luigi Nervi	36
Avenue du Maréchal Fayolle Housing / 62	SANAA	166
Bourse de Commerce – Pinault Collection / 12	Tadao Ando Architect & Associates	52
Centre Georges Pompidou / 14	Renzo Piano, Richard Rogers	56
Chris Marker Student Housing / 23	Experience	78
Cinémathèque Française / 35	Frank Gehry / Atelier de l'île	102
Cité de la musique / 47	Christian de Portzamparc	130
Cité de Refuge – Salvation Army Hostel / 31	Le Corbusier, Pierre Jeanneret	94
Cognacq-Jay Hospital / 79	Toyo Ito	202
Cultural and Sports Center Saint-Blaise / 41	BRUTHER	118
Espaces d'Abraxas / 39	Ricardo Bofill Taller de Arquitectura	114
Fondation Cartier pour l'art contemporain / 20	Jean Nouvel, Emmanuel Cattani & Associés	72
Fondation d'Entreprise Galeries Lafayette / 15	OMA	58
Fondation Jérôme Seydoux Pathé / 19	Renzo Piano Building Workshop	70
Fondation Louis Vuitton / 63	Frank Gehry	168
Gaîté Montparnasse / 21	MVRDV	74
Grande Arche de La Défense / 67	Johann Otto von Spreckelsen	176
Headquarters of the French Communist Party / 44	Oscar Niemeyer, Paul Chemetov	124
Institut du Monde Arabe / 17	Jean Nouvel (lead architect), Gilbert Lézénès, Pierre Soria, Architecture Studio	66
Jean Bouin Stadium / 74	Rudy Ricciotti	192
La Défense: Terrasses Boieldieu / 65	Empreinte, Pierre Gangnet, MAARU, Igrec Ingénierie, L.E.A.	172
La Piscine des Amiraux / 54	Henri Sauvage / Chatillon Architectes (restoration)	146
La Samaritaine / 11	SANAA	50
Le Corbusier's Apartment-Studio / 73	Le Corbusier	190
Le Monde Group Headquarters / 33	Snøhetta, SRA Architectes	98
***le*19M – Fashion Manufactury of Chanel / 49**	Rudy Ricciotti	134
Les Arènes de Picasso / 38	Manuel Núñez Yanowsky	112
Les Choux de Créteil / 37	Gérard Grandval	110
Les Étoiles d'Ivry / 29	Renée Gailhoustet, Jean Renaudie	90
Les Orgues de Flandre / 50	Martin van Treeck	136
Longchamp Racecourse / 71	Dominique Perrault	184
Maine-Montparnasse II Residential Building / 22	Jean Dubuisson	76
Maison de Verre / 02	Pierre Chareau, Bernard Bijvoet	30

Maison des Sciences de l'Homme / 03	Marcel Lods / Chatillon Architectes (restoration)	32
Maison du Brésil / 26	Le Corbusier, Lúcio Costa	84
Maison du Peuple de Clichy / 58	Marcel Lods, Eugène Beaudouin, Jean Prouvé, Vladimir Bodiansky / Jouin Manku, Perrot & Richard Architects (restoration)	154
Maison Jaoul / 64	Le Corbusier	170
Maison La Roche-Jeanneret / 75	Le Corbusier	194
Maison Planeix / 28	Le Corbusier	88
Mallet-Stevens Houses / 76	Robert Mallet-Stevens	196
Meditation Space UNESCO / 04	Tadao Ando Architect & Associates	34
Ministry of Economics and Finance / 34	Paul Chemetov, Borja Huidobro, Louis Arretche, Roman Karasinski	100
Morland Mixité Capitale / 16	David Chipperfield Architects	64
Musée d'Orsay / 01	Gae Aulenti	28
Museé du Louvre (Pyramid and Department of Islamic Arts) / 10	Ieoh Ming Pei (Pyramid) / Rudy Ricciotti, Mario Bellini (Department of Islamic Arts)	46
Musée du Quai Branly / 07	Ateliers Jean Nouvel	40
National Archives of France / 55	Studio Fuksas	148
National Library of France – François-Mitterrand / 32	Dominique Perrault	96
Notre Dame de Pentecôte / 66	Franck Hammoutène	174
Palais de Tokyo – extension / 08	Lacaton & Vassal	42
Parc André-Citroën / 78	Patrick Berger, Gilles Clément	200
Parc de la Villette / 46	Bernard Tschumi	128
Paris Courthouse / 60	Renzo Piano Building Workshop	158
Paris La Défense Arena / 68	Christian de Portzamparc	178
Paris-Saclay / 81	Michel Desvigne, Xaveer De Geyter Architects, Floris Alkemade (masterplan)	206
Passerelle Simone-de-Beauvoir / 36	Dietmar Feichtinger Architects	104
Philharmonie de Paris / 48	Ateliers Jean Nouvel, Métra+Associés (concert hall)	132
Pigalle Duperré / 52	Ill-Studio	142
Pushed Slab / 27	MVRDV	86
Residence for Researchers Julie-Victoire Daubié / 24	BRUTHER	80
Rue de Meaux Housing / 45	Renzo Piano Building Workshop	126
Rue de Ménilmontant Social Housing / 43	Henri Gaudin, Isabelle Marin	122
Saint-Denis Pleyel Railway Station / 56	Kengo Kuma & Associates	150
Site Tour Eiffel / 06	Gustafson Porter + Bowman	38
Social Housing Pelleport / 42	BRUTHER	120
Student Residence / 51	LAN	138
Studios Rive Gauche (ex Canal+ Headquarters) / 77	Richard Meier and Partners	198
Swiss Pavilion / 25	Le Corbusier, Pierre Jeanneret	82
The Olympic and Paralympic Village – Paris 2024 Île-Saint-Denis / 57	Dominique Perrault	152
Tour Bois-le-Prêtre / 59	Raymond Lopez / Frédéric Druot, Lacaton & Vassal	156
Tour Triangle / 80	Herzog & de Meuron	204
Tours Aillaud / 70	Émile Aillaud	182
Tristan Tzara House / 53	Adolf Loos	144
Wood Up Tower / 30	LAN	92
ZAC Le Croissant / 69	Topotek 1	180
ZAC Porte de Vincennes / 40	Topotek 1	116

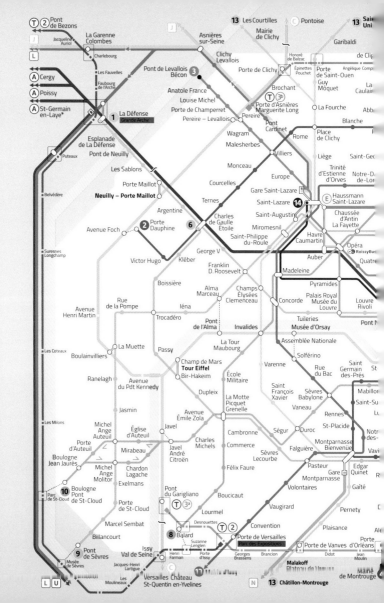

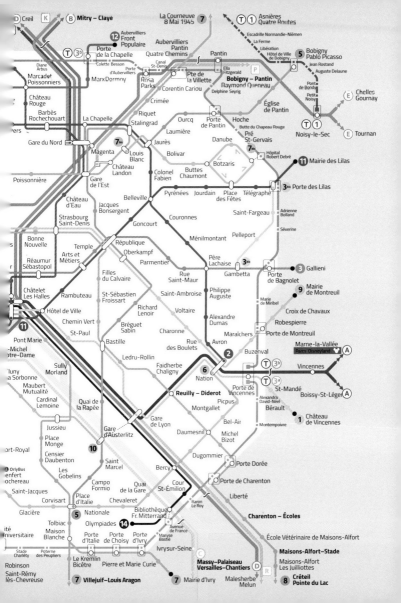

This volume was printed in May 2024
by ABC Tipografia, Calenzano, Florence

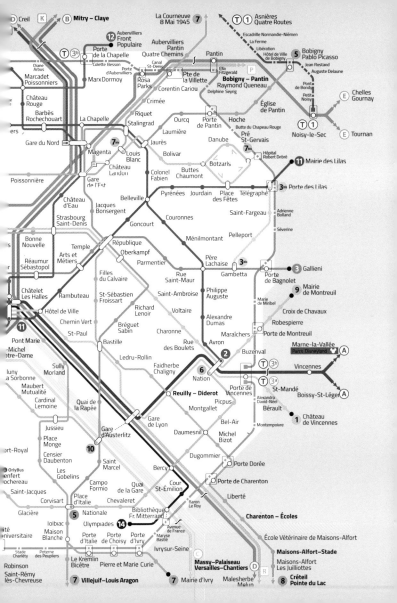

This volume was printed in May 2024
by ABC Tipografia, Calenzano, Florence